FOURTH EDITION

Basic
Music

Functional Musicianship
for the Non-Music Major

Robert E. Nye
Professor of Music
University of Oregon

Bjornar Bergethon
Professor of Music
University of Illinois

733610

PRENTICE-HALL, INC., Englewood Cliffs, New Jersey

Library of Congress Cataloging in Publication Data

NYE, ROBERT EVANS.
  Basic music.

  First-2d eds. published under title: Basic music for
classroom teachers; 3d ed. under title: Basic music, an
activities approach to functional musicianship.
  1. School music—Instruction and study—United
States.   I. Bergethon, Bjornar, joint author.
I. Title.
MT3.U5N9 1973   372.8′7′0973   72-5956
ISBN   0-13-065664-X

Printed in the United States of America

10 9 8 7 6 5 4 3 2

PRENTICE-HALL INTERNATIONAL, INC.,   *London*
PRENTICE-HALL OF AUSTRALIA, PTY. LTD.,   *Sydney*
PRENTICE-HALL OF CANADA, LTD.,   *Toronto*
PRENTICE-HALL OF INDIA PRIVATE LIMITED,   *New Delhi*
PRENTICE-HALL OF JAPAN, INC.,   *Tokyo*

Contents

3

Intervals, Scales, and Chords 50

4

Major Scales and Chording 69

5

Minor Scales and Chording 95

6

The Pentatonic Scale and the Modes 119

7

Harmonizing Songs   128

8

Variety in Piano Chording   133

9

Composing Songs   144

10

Concepts of Musical Form   150

11

Style Periods in Music   162

12

Instruments and Voices   174

appendix A

Hand Signals for Syllable Names   186

appendix B

The Recorder   188

appendix C

The Guitar and Ukulele   193

appendix D

Some Common Musical Terms   198

appendix E

Patriotic Songs   200

Preface

This book is designed for use as a college text in music fundamentals for the general student and for the student who plans to become a classroom teacher in the elementary school. It presents an integrated approach to developing functional musicianship through singing and listening, playing instruments, reading and writing musical notation, analyzing and creating music. The emphasis is on *making music*. Starting with the singing and playing of easy, familiar songs, the student continues to make music in a variety of ways, gaining in musical comprehension and skill through a series of activities which are structured sequentially with regard to difficulty.

Basic concepts of rhythm, melody, harmony, and form are dealt with from the very beginning in a functional manner. Musical terminology and theoretical details are introduced gradually and specifically only as needed, the approach being experience first, explanation later. In this way these aspects of musicianship are learned easily and efficiently because they apply directly to the music at hand, and therefore make sense.

Essential performance skills are developed progressively through a variety of meaningful musical experiences. Specific chapter assignments for *Developing Skills* and *Analytic-Creative Activities* are provided for independent study and reenforcement of musical learnings. Discriminating music listening is developed further in chapters dealing with *Concepts of Musical Form*, *Style Periods in Music*, and *Instruments and Voices*. The repertoire of listening selections included in these chapters will enable the student to expand his musical horizon and to increase his understanding and enjoyment of many types of music.

The Authors

1
Rhythm, Melody, Harmony, and Form

Let us begin our study of basic music by focusing attention on four concepts of musical organization: rhythm, melody, harmony, and form. Through singing and playing a few well-known songs we shall discover how rhythm and melody are interrelated, how they are shaped into formal designs, and how harmony can be used to support the rhythmic structure and add color to the melodic line. At the same time, we shall be developing increasing skill in singing and in playing instruments, in listening to music, and in reading music notation.

RHYTHM OF THE BEAT

Sing the following familiar songs in a manner appropriate to the meaning of the words.

MERRILY WE ROLL ALONG

LOVE SOMEBODY

American Folksong

2. *Love somebody, can't guess who,*
   Love somebody, but I won't tell who.

3. *Love somebody's eyes of blue,*
   Love somebody, but I won't tell who.

4. *Love somebody's smile so true,*
   Love somebody, but I won't tell who.

Clap your hands in time to the music as you sing these songs several times. You will notice there is a steady *beat* or *pulse* that continues uninterrupted throughout the song regardless of whether the tones of the melody are longer or shorter. As you continue to sing and to clap you will observe that the beats fall into a pattern which you can count as "ONE-Two," "ONE-Two," the first being heavy (*accented*) and the second light (*unaccented*).

Love some-bod - y, yes I do,

\>   \>

1   2   1   2

(>) *accent marking*

Emphasize this distinction between the two beats by clapping louder on the accented beat.

Now conduct the songs as you sing by moving your right hand *down* on the accented beat and *up* on the unaccented beat, like this:

Love some-bod - y, yes I do,

\>   \>

1   2   1   2

DOWN   Up   DOWN   Up

The first beat, "ONE," is called the *down-beat* and the second beat, "TWO," is called the *up-beat*.

"Go Tell Aunt Rhody" is another song that moves in twos, although at a somewhat slower pace or *tempo*. Notice in conducting this song that your hand and arm will move slower to accommodate the difference in tempo between this and "Love Somebody."

GO TELL AUNT RHODY

Go tell Aunt Rho - dy, go tell Aunt Rho - dy;

go tell Aunt Rho - dy the old gray goose is dead.

2. The one she's been saving......to make a feather bed,
3. She died in the mill pond......a-standing on her head.
4. The old gander's weeping......because his wife is dead.
5. The goslings are weeping ......because their mother's dead.

RHYTHM OF THE MELODY

As you sing "Go Tell Aunt Rhody" pay particular attention to how the melody moves in relation to the beat. You will notice that not all the tones of the melody fall on the beat: some occur on the beat, others come between beats, and the last note is sustained longer than one beat. The *rhythm of the melody*, therefore, is quite different from the rhythm of the beat because some syllables are sung on short tones while others are sung on longer tones. Sing the song again and observe that the *melody-rhythm* coincides with the *word-rhythm*.

The rhythm of the melody is sometimes symbolized in *line-notation*, which serves as a visual aid to observing the rhythmic features of the melody, i.e., the relative *duration* of the tones within the melody. The melody-rhythm for "Go Tell Aunt Rhody" would look like this in line-notation:

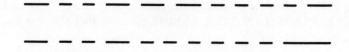

Clap this rhythm while counting the beats, "ONE-Two."

In order to indicate the accent of the first beat we draw a vertical line into the line-notation, thus:

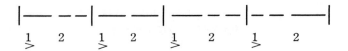

Observe that this line is drawn to the *left* of the line-note on which the accent falls. Insert this vertical line into the other half of the line-notation above for "Go Tell Aunt Rhody"; then clap the melody-rhythm again, accenting the first beat as you count.

The steady beat or pulse is the regulator of the rhythmic movement of the melody. However, every melody has its own rhythmic pattern which becomes a characteristic of that particular melody. Discover this for yourself by comparing the melody-rhythms of "Go Tell Aunt Rhody" and "Love Somebody." Write down the line notation of the latter, in the space provided, for comparison.

Symbols for Duration

Since music is "sound in time," we must have some way of indicating just how long each tone in a melody should be sustained. Line-notation can only indicate approximate *duration*. A more precise way of indicating the relative duration of tones within a melody is to use *notes* of different shapes. If you look at the printed notation for "Go Tell Aunt Rhody," you will see that it has three

differently shaped notes: ♩, ♫, ♩. As you sing the melody and clap the beats while looking at the notation, you will discover that the first kind of note

(♩), called *quarter note*, coincides with the beat while it takes two notes of

the second kind (♫), called *eighth notes,* to equal the duration of a beat, and that the third kind of note ($\textstyle{\frac{1}{4}}$), called *half note*, has a duration of two beats. From this you can see that there is a 1 to 2 relationship between these *note values*, or note durations, which can be expressed as follows:

This relative duration of note values is one of the basic concepts of rhythmic notation which we shall explore further in Chapter 2. For the present, look at the notation again and reinforce your understanding of this concept by clapping the melody-rhythm and tapping the beat rhythm with your foot as you count "ONE-Two," "ONE-Two." Do the same with the following familiar song, "Lightly Row."

LIGHTLY ROW

MELODY AND FORM

As you sing and listen to "Lightly Row," you sense that the melody moves forward toward the tone for the word "go," where it seems to come to a momentary pause; and then, it progresses until it reaches the word "tide," where there is a longer pause. Such pauses in the melody are called *cadences*, and a cadence marks the end of a musical *phrase*. A phrase may be likened to a musical comment or thought; cadences act as musical punctuation marks to conclude phrases. In songs, phrases often correspond to the lines of the poetry. Thus there are four phrases in "Lightly Row."

1. Lightly row, lightly row, o'er the glassy waves we go;

2. Smoothly glide, smoothly glide, on the silent tide.

3. Let the winds and waters be mingled with our melody;

4. Sing and float, sing and float, in our little boat.

Listen to the separate phrases. Can you hear that three of them are almost alike? Which one is different from the others? How do the four phrases differ from each other? If you can hear such similarities and differences in the phrase structure of music, you have sensed the essence of *form* in music. Form embodies *unity* and *variety;* unity can be represented by repetition of like or near-like phrases; variety can be supplied by contrasting phrases.

The arrangement of the phrases in "Lightly Row" is called a *three-part song form* or an *ABA* form. (While AABA would be a more accurate description of this form, it is customary to use ABA as its abbreviation.) "Go Tell Aunt Rhody" is an example of the *two-part song form* or *AB* form. What is the essential difference between these two forms?

An awareness of form is especially helpful in learning and memorizing new songs; it is also useful in many other musical activities, as you will find in succeeding chapters.

MELODIC CONTOUR

The melody of "Whistle, Daughter, Whistle" consists of one single phrase and its repetition.

WHISTLE, DAUGHTER, WHISTLE

With mock seriousness
American Folksong

Mother :
Whis-tle, Daugh-ter, whis-tle, and you shall have a cow.

Daughter:
I can't whis-tle, Moth-er, you nev-er taught me how.

2. Whistle, Daughter, whistle, and you shall have a goat.
   I can't whistle, Mother, because it hurts my throat.

3. Whistle, Daughter, whistle, and you shall have a pig.
   I can't whistle, Mother, because I am too big.

4. Whistle, Daughter, whistle, you shall have a man.
   (whistle   ), I'll do the best I can.

A melody is a succession of tones, or *pitches,* the movement of which is governed by rhythm. Pitch is a term that refers to the relative highness or lowness of a tone. As you listen to the melody of "Whistle, Daughter, Whistle," your ear will tell you that the tones move in three ways, upward, downward, or stay on the same level, like this:

Whis-tle, Daugh-ter, whis-tle, and you shall have a cow.

Tonal movement and direction are important concepts of melodic organization that should be emphasized in early musical experiences.

Melodic contour can be visualized in various ways. One way of doing this is to use hand motions to show how successive tones sound higher or lower or stay in the same place. As you sing the melody, hold your hand in front of you, palm down, and raise or lower the hand to match the relative height of the tones. Another way is to use line-notation to represent these *pitch levels,* as well as their duration. The line-notation for "Whistle, Daughter, Whistle" looks like this:

— — — — — — — — — — — —

Practice singing this melody on a neutral syllable such as "loo," with hand motions. Next, act out the melodic direction with your hand silently; close your eyes and *think* the melody apart from any sounds. Do this several times until you truly feel the pitch levels of the separate tones in the melody. Do the same with other songs.

7

PITCH NOTATION

Line-notation as a device for indicating the exact pitches of a melody has its limitations. For a more precise method of doing this we must use the conventional notation system which employs notes in combination with a *music staff.* We have already observed how different kinds of notes may be used to symbolize the relative duration of the tones in a melody. These same notes can also be used as symbols for exact pitches when they are placed on a music staff.

The staff consists of five lines and four spaces which are numbered upward from the bottom:

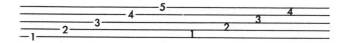

Each line and each space has its own *pitch name* derived from the musical "alphabet" which employs only seven letters: A B C D E F G. These can be visualized on a piano keyboard:

PIANO KEYBOARD

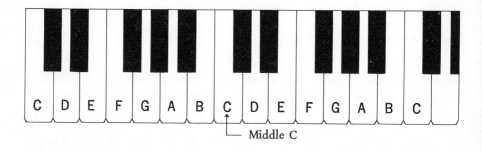

— Middle C

As you look at this keyboard you will see that the white and black keys are arranged so that the black keys fall into groups of twos and threes. The white key to the left of the two black keys is C and the key by that name in the center of the keyboard is called *middle C.* We shall refer to this key again as we continue our explanation of pitch notation.

The pitch names for the lines and spaces are determined by a *clef sign* which is placed at the beginning of the staff. The two most commonly used clefs are the *treble clef* (𝄞) and the *bass clef* (𝄢). The treble clef is also called the *G clef* because it designates the pitch name for the *second* line of the staff as "G" above middle C.

8

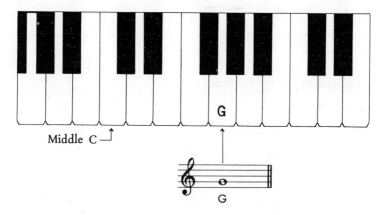

Middle C

G

Using this clef as a point of orientation we can now name the lines and spaces of the treble staff:

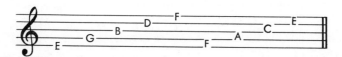

The treble staff is used to notate music that is intended for relatively high-pitched voices and instruments: children's and women's voices, flute, oboe, clarinet, saxophone, trumpet, French horn, and violin.

The bass clef is also called the *F clef* because it designates the pitch name for the *fourth* line of the staff as "F" below middle C.

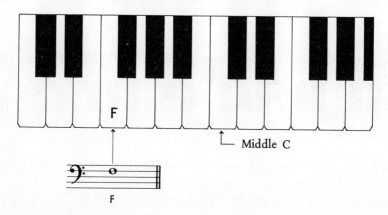

F

Middle C

F

The names of the lines and spaces of the *bass staff* are:

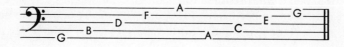

9

The bass staff is used primarily for music intended for lower-pitched voices and instruments: men's voices, bassoon, trombone, baritone, tuba, cello, string bass, and tympani.

Short lines above or below the staff are called *leger lines*. Middle C is on the first leger line below the treble staff.

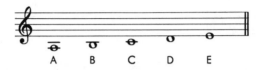

Middle C is also on the first leger line above the bass staff.

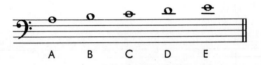

When the treble and bass staffs are used together, they form a *grand staff* of eleven lines with the middle C leger line in the center.

THE GRAND STAFF

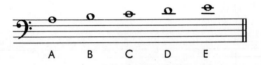

The grand staff is used for music written for the piano, organ, harp, and celeste.

Reading Pitch Notation

Teachers use different approaches for introducing children to the reading of pitch notation. Some will use the letter names of the pitches (A, B, C, D, E, F, G); others may use number names (1, 2, 3, 4, 5, 6, 7, 8) or syllable names (*do, re, me, fa, so, la, ti, do*); many use all three approaches. Whichever names are used, they will most often be related to a scale pattern, usually the familiar *major* scale.[1] Sing this scale ascending and descending in all three ways:

THE C SCALE

C	D	E	F	G	A	B	C	C	B	A	G	F	E	D	C
1	2	3	4	5	6	7	8	8	7	6	5	4	3	2	1
do	re	mi	fa	so	la	ti	do	do	ti	la	so	fa	mi	re	do

This is called the scale of C because it begins and ends on C.

If you look at the notation of the songs in this chapter, you will see that all the tones in the melodies belong to this C scale; therefore, we say that these songs are in the *key of C*.

Singing with Numbers and Syllables

The first two phrases of "Lightly Row" would be sung like this with number names:

Phrase 1:   5 3 3— 4 2 2— 1 2 3 4 5 5 5—

Phrase 2:   5 3 3— 4 2 2— 1 3 5 5 3———

Phrase 3:

Phrase 4:

With syllable names they would be sung like this:[2]

Phrase 1:   s m m— f r r— d r m f s s s—

Phrase 2:   s m m— f r r— d m s s m———

Phrase 3:

Phrase 4:

Write down the remaining phrases in the same manner and sing "Lightly Row" in both ways with hand motions.

---

[1] Scales and their construction will be discussed in Chapter 3.
[2] The single letter for the syllable names is a "shorthand" method used in many European countries. Also, in certain of these countries *hand signals* are used to denote the degrees of the scale. These hand signals can be found in Appendix A.

Many people are fortunate in that they have had a great deal of experience in singing, enjoy it, and are confident about it. Others may have to work to remedy deficiencies in their childhood education which have left them with a few problems in the use of their voices.

Occasionally a person may not have been helped to listen carefully to pitches and pitch changes. As we know, pitches can repeat, move up, or move down. Sometimes they move stepwise and sometimes they move by skips. By listening carefully to these aspects of pitch, and by playing familiar songs on bells or piano, individuals can help themselves to improved hearing. With practice in playing such songs on these keyboard instruments they can eventually sing the pitches they play and can feel the distance between pitches as they play them. Later they can sing the songs without the aid of an instrument.

Sometimes the major difficulty is the voice range. The songs thus far have been placed in the easiest range for beginning group singing, and performing them should be no problem for anyone. However, songs later on in this book will have a wider range. If some of these seem "too high," the singer may be using only the lower part of his natural range, the "chest voice," and he needs to discover and learn to use the higher part of his natural range, the "head voice." Students who have never used this higher voice may quite properly find themselves sounding like young children's singing until there has been time to develop this new voice. *Those who already know that their voices are "too low" should begin now to find and develop the head voice* in order to be able to utilize their full vocal range. The way to begin is to imitate the voice of the young child, as suggested above.

The voice quality most pleasing is a natural-sounding one in which there is no evidence of strain or discomfort. There will be breath support to sustain the tone. Voice quality will vary to some extent in accordance with the meaning of the words of songs. For example, the type of tone desirable in a lullaby would be different than the tone desired in a stirring patriotic song. A relaxed throat is always recommended. Teachers commonly ask for "an open, relaxed mouth and throat."

The musical phrase should not be broken by taking a breath; the singer plans for sufficient breath to complete the phrase. Of course, words should never be broken by attempting to take a breath between syllables. Often the punctuation gives the singer direction as to where to breathe; usually one sings as he speaks, with regard to breathing. Tones are *attacked* and *released* in accordance with the notated music. It helps to remember that singing is only sustained speech; we sing vowels and sustain them; consonants are usually only a form of punctuation separating the vowels.

PLAYING MELODIES

Various types of simple melody instruments may be used to help reinforce aural concepts of melodic organization and to further the ability to read music notation. Of the many instruments available for classroom use we have chosen the *Resonator Bells*[3] and the *piano* for our purpose.[4]

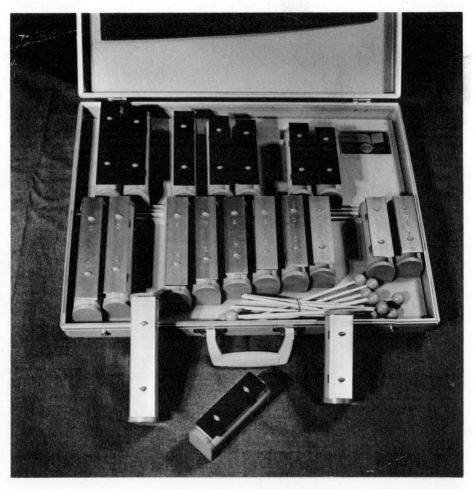

Resonator Bells. Model M.E.G. 500. *Music Education Group.*

[3] Mallet-played instruments of various types are available in many sizes and price ranges. Some of the more popular instruments are the *Step Bells,* the *Song Bells* or *Tone Bells,* and the *xylophone.*
[4] Blowing type instruments such as the Flutophone, Recorder, Song Flute, and Tonette are also useful for playing melodies. See Appendix B for information about the Recorder.

A unique feature of the Resonator Bells is that the tonebars are mounted separately so that the player can choose whichever ones are needed for any given purpose.

Note that the white and black bars are arranged like the piano keyboard and that the names of the pitches are stamped into the metal bars. This makes it easy to select those needed to play a particular melody. The songs we have been singing in this chapter utilized only the following pitches: C D E F G. Remove these bars from the case and arrange them in order from *low* to *high* pitches, like this:

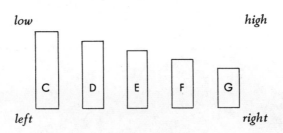

As you play the melodies on these bells, you will become aware of an important concept concerning keyboard-type instruments: that tones which go "up" are played by moving to the *right* and that tones which go "down" are played by moving to the *left*.

It is very easy to play these same melodies on the piano. Find middle C and place the thumb of your right hand on this key; then play the tones C D E F G successively with the five fingers this way:

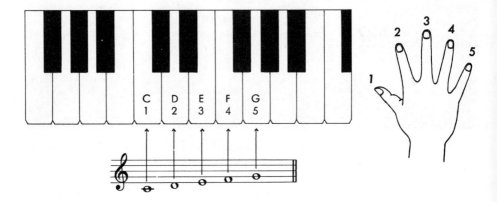

You should have no difficulty in playing the melodies on the piano if you keep your hand in this five-finger position.

14

If you would like to play the melodies with the left hand, you should place the little finger of this hand on C in order to be in a convenient five-finger position. Choosing the C below middle C for the left hand makes it possible to play the melodies with both hands together. Try this.

PLAYING ACCOMPANIMENTS

Accompaniments add interest and color to the singing and playing of songs. One very effective, yet simple, type of accompaniment which is used frequently is called "chording." A *chord* is a combination of several tones, usually three or more, sounded together. Chords produce *harmony*, and a succession of chords creates *harmonic movement*. Harmony gives coloristic support to the melody and reinforces the rhythmic movement as well. The Autoharp[5] and the piano are both suitable for chording.[6]

Autoharp. Model 21C. *Courtesy Oscar Schmidt International, Inc.*

[5] The Autoharp comes in various models: 5-bar, 12-bar, and 15-bar. The 15-bar is the most popular today.
[6] Other chording instruments are the ukulele and the guitar. See Appendix C.

Autoharp Chording

Place the Autoharp on a table or desk or in your lap so that the corner of the two straight sides points toward the body. With the left-hand index finger firmly press down the button marked "C Maj," and stroke the strings from left to right with the right hand, using a hard felt or celluloid pick. The stroke should cover the full range of strings. Next, press the button marked "G_7" with the middle finger and stroke the strings as before. Practice pressing the buttons and stroking, alternately, until you can change from one *chord* to another easily. In doing so, familiarize yourself with the sound of each chord.

You now have two chords that can be used for creating accompaniments to the songs you have been singing and playing. Look at the notation for these songs and you will see that the chords to be used are indicated above the staff. Different people will have different ideas here, but most of you will stroke on the same beats you clapped a while ago; others may want to chord only on "ONE" and rest on "two."

Chord Names

Chords receive their names from the tones of the scale upon which they are built. All the melodies you have sung and played in this chapter are in the key of C. The Autoharp chords that you used to accompany these songs also belong to the key of C. The first chord, "C," is called *C chord* or *I chord* because it is built on the first degree of the C scale. The second chord is called G_7 *chord* or V_7 *chord* because it is built on the fifth degree of the scale. The lowest tone of such chord is called the *chord root* and, therefore, the chord receives its name from its *root*, the pitch name or number of the scale tone on which it is built.

The I chord is also called *tonic chord* because its chord root is the *tonic* or 1 of the scale. The fifth step of the scale is called *dominant* and, therefore, the V_7 chord also goes by the name of *dominant seventh chord*.

Piano Chording

Chording can be done in several ways on the piano. One would be to play the chords as notated above with the right hand. The three tones of the I chord could be played in the five-finger position you used for playing the melodies. For the V_7 chord you would have to place the thumb on G and then play the other notes with index, ring, and little fingers. If you were to play these chords with the left hand, they would probably be notated in the bass clef, like this:

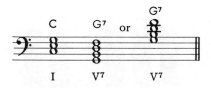

Find these chords on the piano keyboard.

In trying to play the chords as notated above you probably discovered that you have had to move your hand a great deal. However, there is a much easier way to play the I–V_7 progression which will enable you to add piano accompaniments to songs much more readily. For the present we shall limit ourselves to chording with the left hand only.

Place the little finger of your left hand on the C-key below middle C, the middle finger on the E-key, and the thumb on the G-key. When you play these three keys simultaneously, you are playing the C chord.

THE C CHORD

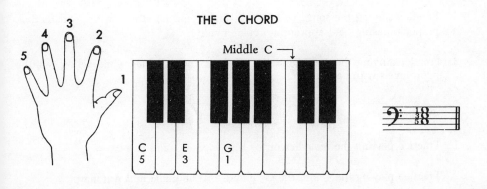

The G_7 chord is played from the C–E–G position in the following manner: move the little finger down to the B-key; place the index finger on the F-key; and leave the thumb on the G-key, as before. Playing the B–F–G together produces the G_7 chord.[7]

THE G^7 CHORD

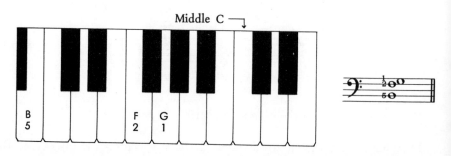

Practice playing these two chords alternately until you get the feel of the chord changes. After you have achieved some facility in doing this, you will be able to play all the songs in this chapter with the melody in the right hand together with the accompaniment in the left hand without much difficulty.

DEVELOPING SKILLS

Singing

1. Practice singing the songs with words, giving special attention to good diction, proper phrasing, and appropriate voice quality.

2. Practice singing the melodies with numbers and syllables while acting out the pitch levels with hand motions.

Playing

1. Practice playing the melodies on bells, xylophone, and piano.

2. Practice playing the C and the G_7 chords on the piano and Autoharp.

---

[7] Note that the fourth tone of the G_7 chord, D, has been left out; this can be done without altering the quality of this chord. A more detailed discussion of the I and V_7 chords will be given in Chapter 3.

3. Practice playing the melodies and the chords together on the piano.

4. Experiment at the piano by playing the melody with the left hand (in the bass) and the chords with the right hand.

Reading

1. Practice naming the following pitches:

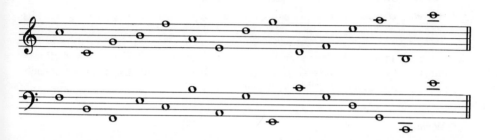

2. Practice singing the following tonal sequences with letter names, numbers, and syllables:

3. Practice clapping the following rhythmic phrases:

4. Make up groups of players and perform two or more of the above rhythmic phrases together as *duets, trios,* or *quartets.* Use different instruments for each part (drums, sticks, woodblock, triangle, etc.).

Writing

1. Practice drawing treble and bass clef signs.

2. Practice writing the notes found in the songs (♩, ♩, ♫) and placing them on the staff, using the following rules as guides:
   a. Notes have the following properties: *note head* ("black" or "open"), *stem,* and *flag.* When flags are joined together, they are called *beams.*

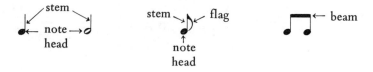

b. Note heads are placed on the lines or in the spaces of the staff for the pitches desired.

c. Stems may extend upward or downward. A note on the third line of the staff may have its stem either upward or downward:

A note below this line has its stem extended upward and a note above this line has its stem extended downward.

If the stem extends upward, it is placed to the right of the note; if it extends downward, it is placed to the left of the note; see above.

3. Complete writing the indicated pitches with the same kind of notes:

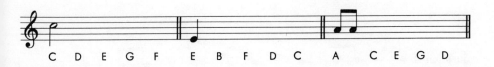

C   D   E   G   F   E   B   F   D   C   A   C   E   G   D

4. Complete transcribing the notation of "Go Tell Aunt Rhody" to the bass clef:

Vocabulary

Practice defining or explaining the following musical terms:

accent	form	pitch
beat	grand staff	rhythm
cadence	harmony	staff
chord	key	tempo
clef	leger line	tone
conduct	melody	tonic
dominant	note	three-part form
down-beat	phrase	two-part form
duration		

ANALYTIC-CREATIVE ACTIVITIES

1. Create several different rhythmic patterns based on ♩., ♩ and ♫ and present these to the class. Establish the underlying beat and have the class repeat the patterns like an "echo."

2. Experiment with "question and answer" clapping or drumming. One person may create (improvise) the question and another can be called upon to improvise an answer.

Example:

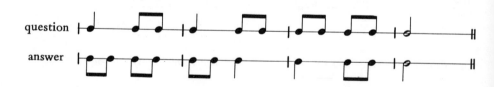

3. On which tones of the scale of C do the melodies of the songs in this chapter begin and end? Are these tones related to the I chord? How?

4. Study the melodies to see in which direction they move. Is there a change of direction within a phrase? Do the phrases begin on the same tone of the scale? Are any tonal patterns within the phrases repeated?

22

5. Using the knowledge obtained through 3 and 4 above, create a melody phrase of your own based on the tones of the C chord (C, E, G). Use quarter, eighth, and half notes.

6. Using your knowledge of two-part form (see "Go Tell Aunt Rhody"), create a two-part form melody using the five tones of the scale: C, D, E, F, and G.

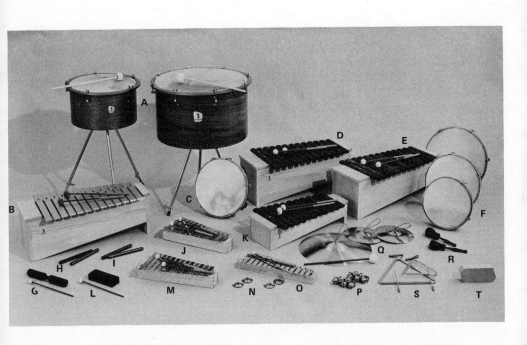

STUDIO 49 Orff Instruments: (A) timpani, (B) alto metallophone, (C) tambourine, (D) bass xylophone, (E) alto xylophone, (F) hand drums, (G) tubular woodblock, (H), (I) claves, (J) soprano glockenspiel, (K) soprano xylophone, (L) woodblock, (M) alto glockenspiel, (N) finger cymbals, (O) soprano metallophone, (P) felt mallett, (Q) cymbals, (R) castanets, (S) triangles, (T) box rattle. *Photograph courtesy of Magnamusic-Baton Inc., St. Louis, Mo. 63130.*

2

Musical Meter and Rhythmic Notation

Almost all of the music you are likely to come into contact with gives the impression of moving in accent groupings of twos or threes; that is, you can count "ONE-Two" or "ONE-Two-Three" as you listen to or perform the music. The songs in the previous chapter afforded you experience with "two-beat" rhythm. Here are two songs exemplifying "three-beat" rhythm.

SUSIE, LITTLE SUSIE[1]

Allegretto[2]

German Folksong

Su - sie, lit - tle Su - sie, now here is some news! Geese are run-ning bare - foot be - cause they've no shoes. The

---

[1] The numbers over the notes are suggested fingerings for playing the melody on the piano: 1-thumb, 2-index finger, 3-middle finger, 4-ring finger, 5-little finger.
[2] *Allegretto* means lively. See Appendix D.

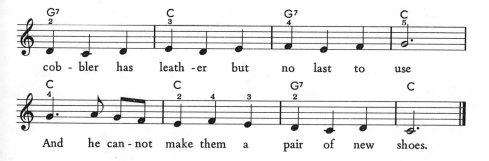

cob - bler   has   leath - er   but   no   last   to   use

And   he can - not   make them   a   pair   of   new   shoes.

MUSICAL METER

As you sing "Susie, Little Susie" and clap the rhythm of the beat, you will feel the beats falling into accent groupings which you can count as "ONE-Two-Three," "ONE-Two-Three," the first beat being accented and the second and third unaccented.

Su	— sie	lit-tle	Su —	sie,	now	here	is	some
>			>			>		
1	2	3	1	2	3	1	2	3

The way you conduct three-beat rhythm is: "DOWN-Right-Up."

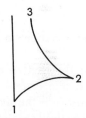

The down-beat, ONE, is heavy and the other beats are light. Practice this conducting pattern as you sing the song again.

"How Does My Lady's Garden Grow?" is another song in which the beat-rhythm falls into accent groupings of threes.

HOW DOES MY LADY'S GARDEN GROW?

Flowingly   English Tune

How   does   my   la - dy's   gar - den   grow?

How   does   my   la - dy's   gar - den   grow?   With

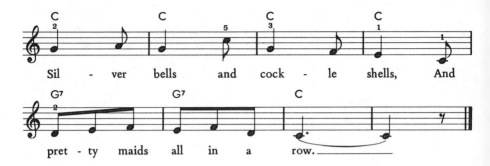

Sil - ver bells and cock - le shells, And
pret - ty maids all in a row.

This melody may not be familiar to you and you may have to learn it with the help of the bells or the piano. All the tones in this song belong to the scale of C which you already know. Review what you learned about this and the names for the various scale degrees (see p. 11). The letter names might be particularly helpful because they are easy to associate with both the notation and the instrument. Try this.

Next, scan the words of the song and note how the word-rhythm (melody-rhythm) and beat-rhythm are related:

How does my	la - dy's	gar - den	grow?
>	>	>	>
1 2 3	1 2 3	1 2 3	1 2 3

After you have learned the song, practice singing it with the three-beat conducting pattern.

By now you have learned that the rhythm of the beat falls into regularly recurring groups of accented and unaccented beats. These repeated groups of beats, or accent groupings, constitute the *meter* in music. When a melody moves in groups of two beats, it is in *duple meter;* when it moves in three beats, it is *triple meter.* Other groupings of beats are possible, as we shall discover farther on.

RHYTHMIC NOTATION

As you sang and played the songs in this and the preceding chapter, you may have observed that the notation of the melodies contained other symbols for duration than those discussed in connection with "Go Tell Aunt Rhody." (see p. 4.) All such symbols are related and belong to our system of rhythmic notation which includes *notes, rests,* and *meter signatures.* Familiarity with these symbols is essential for interpreting the musical score.

Duration of Notes and Rests

Rhythm concerns the duration of sounds (tones) and silences (rests) controlled by an underlying beat or pulsation. The duration (*time values*) of these sounds and silences are symbolized in notation by notes and rests of various shapes:

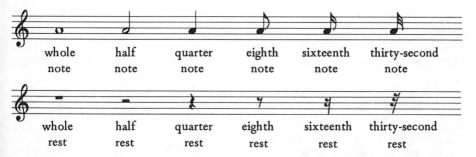

These symbols do not represent exact durations of sounds and silences; they only indicate relationships. The *relative duration* of the notes (note or time values) may be seen from this:

The relative duration of the equivalent rest values would be the same.

Ties and Dots

Tones may be prolonged by connecting two notes of the same pitch with a curved line called a *tie:*[3]

The second note is not sounded separately; the first pitch is merely sustained for the total value of the two notes.

---

[3] When two notes of different pitches are connected, both are sounded and these notes are said to be *slurred:*

A *dot* after a note or a rest increases its value one half:

$$\text{𝅗𝅥.} = \text{𝅗𝅥} + \text{♩} \qquad \blacksquare\text{.} = \blacksquare + \text{𝄽}$$

$$\text{♩.} = \text{♩} + \text{♪} \qquad \text{𝄽.} = \text{𝄽} + \text{𝄾}$$

$$\text{♪.} = \text{♪} + \text{𝅘𝅥𝅯} \qquad \text{𝄾.} = \text{𝄾} + \text{𝄿}$$

$$\text{𝅘𝅥𝅯.} = \text{𝅘𝅥𝅯} + \text{𝅘𝅥𝅰} \qquad \text{𝄿.} = \text{𝄿} + \text{𝅀}$$

Meter or Time Signature

In music notation, the rhythmic flow of tones and rests is measured off into equal time intervals by vertical lines drawn through the staff. These are called *bar lines,* and the note and rest values contained between two such lines make up a *measure.* A *double bar* is used to denote the ending of a song or an instrumental composition or the ending of a section of a lengthy musical work.[4]

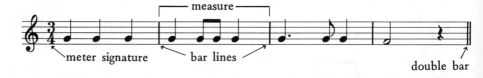

meter signature   bar lines   double bar

At the beginning of the notation of a song or instrumental composition there are two numbers, one above the other, which are referred to as the *meter signature* or *time signature*. The lower number of this signature represents a note value, usually one that represents the *beat unit,* and the upper number indicates the number of such notes, or their equivalents, which are to be found in each measure. In the above illustration the meter signature is $\frac{3}{4}$. This tells

us that the beat unit is a quarter note (♩) and that each measure will contain three such notes, or their equivalents. In other words, each measure is

usually made up of three quarter note beats (♩ ♩ ♩). A three-beat measure is an example of triple meter which is made up of accent groupings of "ONE-

---

[4] Two types of double bars are used: between sections within a composition two light lines are used (‖); at the end of the composition one light and one heavy line is used (‖).

Two-Three." Note that this gives added meaning to the function of the bar lines: it divides the music into metric units of accented and unaccented beats. The beat following the bar line is accented and the beat preceding the bar line is unaccented.

The songs which we have sung and played thus far have exemplified the use of these meter signatures: $\frac{2}{4}$, $\frac{3}{4}$, and $\frac{3}{8}$. Examine the songs again and note the function of the signatures.

$\frac{2}{4}$ indicates two beats to the measure and that a quarter note (𝅘𝅥) will receive one beat ($\frac{2}{\text{𝅘𝅥}}$).

Example: "Love Somebody," p. 2.

$\frac{3}{4}$ indicates three beats to the measure and that a quarter note (𝅘𝅥) will receive one beat ($\frac{3}{\text{𝅘𝅥}}$).

Example: "Susie, Little Susie," p. 24.

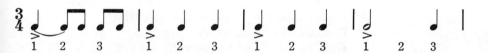

$\frac{3}{8}$ indicates three beats to the measure and that an eighth note (𝅘𝅥𝅮) will receive one beat ($\frac{3}{\text{𝅘𝅥𝅮}}$).

Example: "How Does My Lady's Garden Grow?," p. 25.

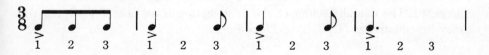

29

Another common meter signature is $\frac{4}{4}$ which indicates that there is to be four beats in the measure and that a quarter note will receive one beat ($\frac{4}{\quarternote}$). A melody which moves in fours is said to be in *quadruple meter*. "A

Cradle Hymn" is an example of such a melody.

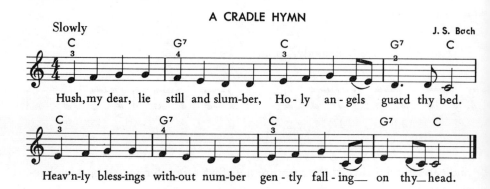

A CRADLE HYMN

Slowly   J. S. Bach

Hush, my dear, lie still and slum-ber, Ho - ly an - gels guard thy bed.

Heav'n-ly bless-ings with-out num-ber gen - tly fall - ing— on thy— head.

    2. *How much better thou'rt attended*
       Than the Son of God could be,
       When from heaven He descended
       And became a child like thee.

    3. *Mayest thou like to know and fear Him,*
       Trust and love Him all thy days,
       Then go dwell forever near Him
       See His face and sing His praise.

Words by Isaac Watts

As you sing this song, you will sense that both the first and third beats are accented, although there seems to be less "stress" on the third beat than on the first. We say there is a *primary accent* on the first beat and a *secondary accent* on the third beat. The second and fourth beats will be felt to be unaccented. The overall feeling of the beat-rhythm is an accent grouping that may be counted as "ONE-Two-*Three*-Four."

Hush, my dear, lie   still and slum - ber

$\frac{4}{4}$ 1 2 3 4 | 1 2 3 4 |

30

You conduct four beats in the following manner: "DOWN-Left-*Right*-Up."

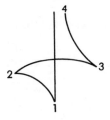

"White Coral Bells" also moves in fours. Practice the four-beat conducting pattern by leading two groups of singers in this favorite two-part round.

WHITE CORAL BELLS

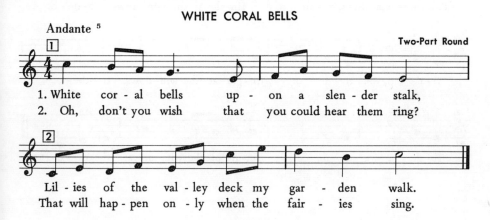

1. White cor - al bells up - on a slen - der stalk,
2. Oh, don't you wish that you could hear them ring?

Lil - ies of the val - ley deck my gar - den walk.
That will hap - pen on - ly when the fair - ies sing.

Sometimes a $\frac{4}{4}$ meter signature may be represented by a symbol which looks like a capital "C." This symbol (**C**) is interchangeable with $\frac{4}{4}$ (see p. 90).

Simple Meters

The meters discussed so far, duple, triple, and quadruple, are called *simple meters* in contradistinction to *compound meters* which we shall consider next. Before concluding our discussion of simple meters we must call attention to another meter signature that is often used to represent duple meter. This is the $\frac{2}{2}$ signature which indicates that there should be two beats in the measure and that a half note (♩) will receive one beat ($\overset{2}{♩}$). Sometimes the symbol (**¢**) will be used to represent $\frac{2}{2}$ meter, in which case it is called *alla breve*.

---

⁵ *Andante* means moderately slow. See Appendix D.

The conductor's beat for $\frac{2}{2}$ is the same as for $\frac{2}{4}$.

JINGLE AT THE WINDOWS

Moderato

Singing Game

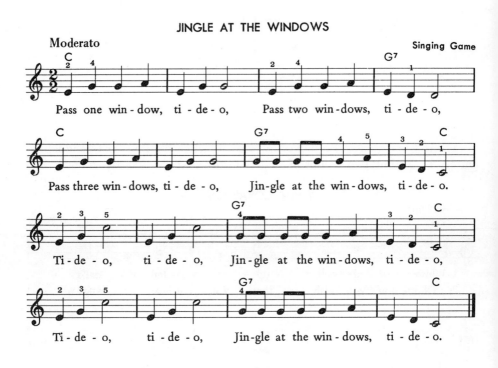

Pass one win - dow, ti - de - o,   Pass two win - dows, ti - de - o,

Pass three win - dows, ti - de - o,   Jin - gle at the win - dows, ti - de - o.

Ti - de - o,   ti - de - o,   Jin - gle at the win - dows, ti - de - o,

Ti - de - o,   ti - de - o,   Jin - gle at the win - dows, ti - de - o.

COME, FOLLOW ME

Gaily

John Hilton

Come, fol - low,   fol - low, fol - low,   Fol - low, fol - low,   fol - low me!

Whith - er shall I   fol - low, fol - low, fol - low, Whith - er shall I fol - low, fol - low thee?

To   the green - wood, to the green - wood, To the green - wood, green - wood tree.

The meter signature does not always indicate the proper number of beats to be found in a measure. For example, the meter signature for "Row, Row, Row Your Boat" is $\frac{6}{8}$ which might indicate that there should be six beats in each measure and that an eighth note (♪) should receive one beat ($\frac{6}{\text{♪}}$).

ROW, ROW, ROW YOUR BOAT

Row, row, row your boat Gent- ly down the stream.____

Mer -ri - ly, mer-ri - ly, mer-ri - ly, mer- ri - ly, Life is but a dream.____

But, when you sing this familiar round, you do not ordinarily feel six beats to the measure, only two. In other words, the dotted quarter note (♩.) becomes the beat unit rather than the eighth note, and this gives you a feeling of duple meter:

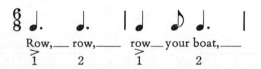

However, as you sing the last phrase you can feel an underlying pulsation of "three" within the dotted quarter note beat unit.

Thus $\frac{6}{8}$ meter is in reality two meters of three pulsations combined to form a meter of six pulsations. For this reason $\frac{6}{8}$ meter gives the impression of having two accented beats. The first beat is marked by a strong, *primary accent*, while the fourth beat has a weaker, *secondary accent*.

33

A combination of two simple (triple) meters such as this is called *compound duple meter, i.e.*, a meter with two beats, each divided into three equal pulsations. Other compound meters are $\frac{9}{8}$ called *compound triple meter*

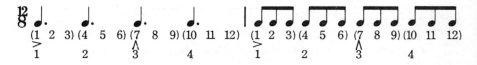

and $\frac{12}{8}$ meter, called *compound quadruple meter*

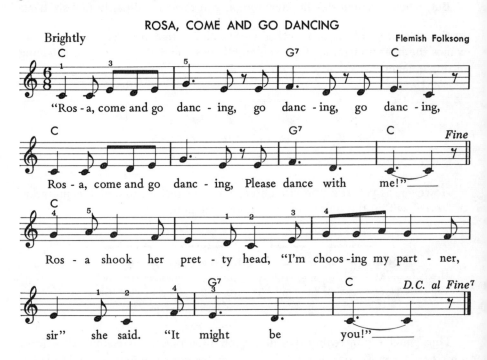

but these are used only infrequently in the song literature for elementary schools.[6]

Our next song, "Rosa, Come and Go Dancing," is also in $\frac{6}{8}$ meter. Although it moves at a more leisurely pace than "Row, Row, Row Your Boat," it still gives a feeling of moving in twos rather than in sixes.

ROSA, COME AND GO DANCING

Brightly

Flemish Folksong

"Ros - a, come and go danc - ing, go danc - ing, go danc - ing,

Ros - a, come and go danc - ing, Please dance with me!"

Ros - a shook her pret - ty head, "I'm choos -ing my part - ner,

sir" she said. "It might be you!"

---

[6] For a song in $\frac{9}{8}$ meter, see "Down in the Valley" (p. 76).

[7] *D.C. al Fine,* from the beginning to *Fine,* the end. See Appendix D.

The conducting pattern most often used for $\frac{6}{8}$ meter is the same as that used for $\frac{2}{4}$ meter, "DOWN-Up," with the heavier down-beat on the primary accent and the lighter up-beat on the secondary accent. However, some songs move at such a slow pace that they require a different conducting pattern, one in which each of the six pulses (eighth notes) within the $\frac{6}{8}$ meter is felt. Our next song, "Cradle Song," is such a song. The six-beat pattern is conducted in this way: DOWN-Left-Left-*Right*-Right-Up.

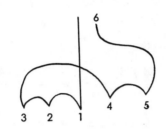

CRADLE SONG

French Folksong

Breez - es blow - ing ev - er so soft - ly, Rock and lull us

gent - ly to sleep. Morn-ing will come with soft glow-ing light;

Then will the ris - ing sun o - ver-come night. Breez - es blow - ing

ev - er so soft - ly, Rock and lull us gent -ly to sleep.

35

DIVISIONS OF THE BEAT UNIT

The various beat units (𝅗𝅥 , 𝅗𝅥., ♩ , ♪) may be divided in many different ways to create interesting rhythmic patterns.

Equal Divisions

In the songs you have had thus far, the quarter and half note beats have usually been divided equally into twos and fours, and the dotted quarter note was divided into threes:

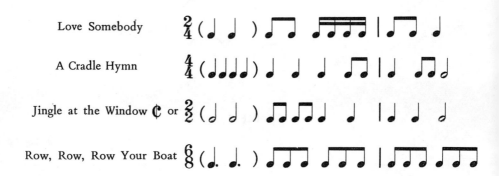

Occasionally there will be *three* notes of equal value within a beat unit which is normally divided into twos:

These notes are called *triplets* and are designated by a number "3" over the notes which are contained within the beat. Therefore, a group of three notes to be played or sung in the place of two of the *same kind* is called a triplet.

"Sing, Sing Together" is an example of a melody containing triplets.

SING, SING TOGETHER

Unequal Divisions

Unequal divisions of the beat unit are also very common. The four sixteenth notes within the quarter note beat may be joined in the following ways to create new rhythmic patterns:

Some of these new rhythmic patterns occur in "Grandma Grunts." Study the notation closely to discover on which beats these occur; then clap the melody-rhythm several times through as you count the beat.

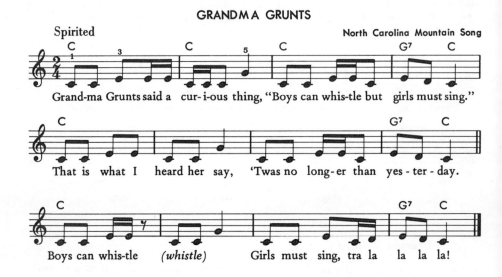

GRANDMA GRUNTS

Spirited

North Carolina Mountain Song

Grand-ma Grunts said a cur-i-ous thing, "Boys can whis-tle but girls must sing."

That is what I heard her say, 'Twas no long-er than yes-ter-day.

Boys can whis-tle (whistle) Girls must sing, tra la la la la!

2. *Boys can whistle, of course they may,*
They can whistle the livelong day.
Why can't girls whistle too, pray tell,
If they manage to do it well?

3. *Grandma Grunts said it wouldn't do,*
Gave a very good reason too:
Whistling girls and crowing hens
Always come to some bad ends.

The three eighth notes within the dotted quarter note beat may be joined in two ways:

$$\text{♩.} = \text{♫♪} = \text{♩ ♪}$$

$$\text{♩.} = \text{♪♫} = \text{♪♩}$$

The first pattern figures prominently in most songs in $\frac{6}{8}$ meter (see "Rosa, Come and Go Dancing"), but the second pattern occurs less frequently, and when it does, it gives a syncopated (see page 41) effect to the rhythm as in the fifth measure of "Hunting Song."

HUNTING SONG

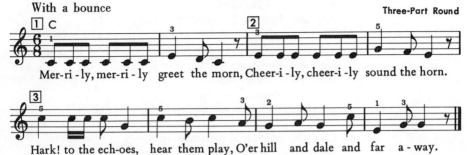

Mer-ri-ly, mer-ri-ly greet the morn, Cheer-i-ly, cheer-i-ly sound the horn.

Hark! to the ech-oes, hear them play, O'er hill and dale and far a-way.

THE UP-BEAT OR ANACRUSIS

All the previous songs have started on the first beat of the measure. However, many songs start on other parts of the measure, usually on the last beat, or on a fraction of the last beat. Such songs are said to begin with an *up-beat* or *anacrusis*. "Billy Boy" begins on the last beat of the measure. Note that the last measure contains only one beat. The reason for this is that when a song begins on an incomplete measure, the last measure will complete this measure.

BILLY BOY

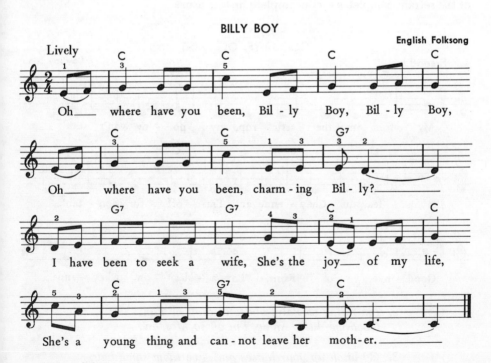

Oh__ where have you been, Bil-ly Boy, Bil-ly Boy,

Oh__ where have you been, charm-ing Bil-ly?_____

I have been to seek a wife, She's the joy__ of my life,

She's a young thing and can-not leave her moth-er._____

2. Did she bid you to come in,
   Billy Boy, Billy Boy?
   Yes, she bid me to come in;
   There's a dimple in her chin:

3. Can she make a cherry pie,
   Billy Boy, Billy Boy?
   She can make a cherry pie,
   quick as cat can wink her eye:

4. Can she cook and can she spin,
   Billy Boy, Billy Boy?
   She can cook and she can spin,
   she can do most anything:

5. How old is she,
   Billy Boy, Billy Boy?
   Three time six and four times seven,
   twenty-eight and eleven:

"Good-Bye, Ol' Paint," which also begins on the last beat of a three-beat measure, has a verse and a refrain. Note that the half note in the last measure of the refrain completes the incomplete first measure.

GOOD-BYE, OL' PAINT

2. I'm riding ol' Paint and a-leading ol' Fan;
   Goodbye, little Annie, I'm off to Montan'.

3. Go hitch up your horses and give them some hay,
   And seat yourself by me as long as you stay.

Observe the double bars with dots at the beginning and end of the refrain. These are *repeat signs* and they indicate that the passage between the two signs should be repeated. If a song or section of a composition is to be repeated from the beginning, only one sign is necessary, the one with dots at the left of the double bar.

When conducting songs that begin with an incomplete measure, the preparatory beat should be given in the direction of the preceding "imaginary" beat.

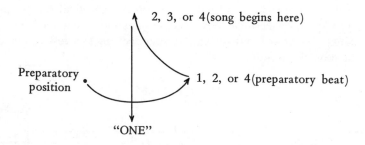

2, 3, or 4(song begins here)

Preparatory position

1, 2, or 4(preparatory beat)

"ONE"

SYNCOPATION

Syncopation is the result of displaced accents within the measure. Accents may be shifted in the following ways:

1. by accenting a normally weak beat.

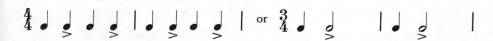

2. by having a rest on a strong beat.

3. by holding a weak beat over a strong beat.

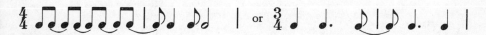

4. by tying a weak portion of a beat to a stronger one.

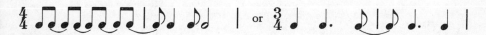

41

The refrain of "Li'l 'Liza Jane" contains two similar, yet somewhat different syncopated patterns:

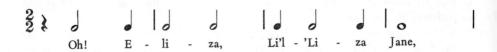

In the first pattern there is a quarter rest on the first beat that must be observed carefully in order to achieve the syncopated effect on "Oh!" As you sing the song, clap your hands or stomp your feet on this rest to avoid a premature entry on the refrain.

LI'L 'LIZA JANE

2. *I got a house in Baltimore, Li'l 'Liza Jane,*
   Brussels carpet on my floor, Li'l 'Liza Jane.

3. *I got a house in Baltimore, Li'l 'Liza Jane,*
   Silver doorplate on my door, Li'l 'Liza Jane.

4. *Come, my love, and marry me, Li'l 'Liza Jane,*
   And I'll take good care of thee, Li'l 'Liza Jane.

"He's Got the Whole World in His Hands" is characterized by a number of interesting syncopation patterns. Study these by clapping the beat and reciting the words first; then clap the melody-rhythm as you count the beat. Note that this song begins on the second half of the third beat.

HE'S GOT THE WHOLE WORLD IN HIS HANDS

2. *He's got the wind and rain in his hands.*

3. *He's got both you and me in his hands.*

By now you have explored most of the metric-rhythm patterns that you are likely to encounter. The following chart may help to summarize what we have learned about musical meter and rhythm in this chapter and also serve as a reference for future use.

DUPLE METER

Beat unit	Metric Pattern	Combined	Divided	Syncopated
$\frac{2}{8}$				
$\frac{2}{4}$				
$\frac{2}{2}$				
$\frac{6}{8}$ Compound duple				

TRIPLE METER

Beat Unit	Metric Pattern	Combined	Divided	Syncopated

(Triple meter: $\frac{3}{8}$, $\frac{3}{4}$, $\frac{3}{2}$, $\frac{9}{8}$ Compound triple — with corresponding notated rhythm patterns)

QUADRUPLE METER

Beat Unit	Metric Pattern	Combined	Divided	Syncopated

(Quadruple meter: $\frac{4}{8}$, $\frac{4}{4}$, $\frac{4}{2}$, $\frac{12}{8}$ Compound quadruple — with corresponding notated rhythm patterns)

DEVELOPING SKILLS

Singing

1. Sing the songs with appropriate expressiveness paying particular attention to rhythmic accuracy, tempo, and phrasing.

2. Practice the conducting patterns for the various meters as you sing the songs.

3. Sing the melodies with number and syllable names.

4. Practice singing and conducting the rounds learned so far with special attention to bringing in the various parts.

5. Try singing "Cradle Song," p. 35, with the syllables while making the appropriate hand signs. See Appendix A.

44

Playing

1. Practice playing the melodies on bells and piano.

2. Practice playing accompaniments on the Autoharp and piano while you or others sing the songs.

3. Practice playing some of the songs with melody and chords together.

4. Add suitable percussion instruments as an accompaniment to singing and playing songs.

Reading

1. Insert bar lines to conform with the meter signatures in the following:

2. Establish a steady beat by counting or tapping the foot and clap the following rhythm patterns. After you have mastered each pattern, clap all the patterns in the same meters in succession without stopping between them.

45

3. After establishing an appropriate beat, count and clap (or play) the following four measure rhythm phrases. Also practice performing them as duets by two individuals or groups, one taking the top line, the other the bottom line. Perform these duets with percussion instruments as well, using a different instrument for each part.

1. Complete the following measures with appropriate notes:

2. Complete the following measures with appropriate rests:

3. Transcribe the notation for "Row, Row, Row Your Boat" to the bass clef.

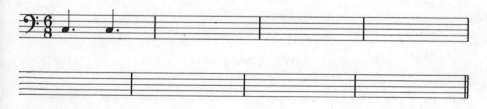

Vocabulary

Define or explain the following musical terms:

anacrusis	meter	slur
bar line	meter signature	syncopation
compound meter	preparatory beat	tie
dot (after note)	quadruple meter	triple meter
duple meter	repeat sign	triplet

ANALYTIC-CREATIVE ACTIVITIES

1. Compare the melody-rhythms of the songs in Chapter 1 by clapping any two of them at the same time.

2. Make up as many rhythmic patterns as you can think of in $\frac{2}{4}$, $\frac{3}{4}$, $\frac{4}{4}$, and $\frac{6}{8}$ meters.

3. Some music has little or no primary accent. Try singing or playing "America" with an accented first beat. Then try it with no accented beats. Which do you prefer? Why?

4. Explore the rhythm of words: names of people, animals, geographical locations, foods, and other subject categories. Notate the rhythm patterns in appropriate meters. Experiment with these, singly and in combinations, in speech and with percussion instruments.

Example:

Moz - art, Hay - dn,   Gluck and Bach;   Schu-mann, Liszt, Rach - ma - ni - noff;

Schu-bert, Strauss and   Of - fen - bach;   Brahms and Rim-sky   Kor - sa - koff.

5. There are three rhythms in every song: the rhythm of the first beat of the measure, the rhythm of the meter, and the rhythm of the melody. Orchestrate these different rhythms of selected songs from Chapters 1 and 2 for percussion instruments.

Example:

LOVE SOMEBODY

(A) Tone block

(B) rhythm sticks

courtesy Peripole, Incorporated

(A) Triangle, (B) gong, (C) maracas, (D) drum, (E) claves, (F) finger cymbals, (G) conga drum, (H) guiro, (I) bongo drums, (J) tambourine, (K) drum. *Photograph courtesy of Tommy Moore, President, Rhythm Band, Incorporated, P.O. Box 126, Fort Worth, Texas.*

3

Intervals, Scales, and Chords

A scale can sometimes take the shape of a melody or part of a melody. Sing "The Swan" in unison and observe that it contains all the tones of the C major scale: C, D, E, F, G, A, B, C.

THE SWAN

Sweet-ly the swan sings, Do-de-ah-do,   do - de-ah-do,   do - de-ah-do.

INTERVALS AND THE MAJOR SCALE

As you sang you probably noticed the wide upward leap between the last note in the first measure and the first note in the second measure: C to C. Although both tones are named C, they obviously represent two different pitches, the second one being higher than the first. The pitch distance between two notes or tones is called an *interval*. Intervals are named according to the number of staff degrees that they encompass. If we count the lines and spaces between the low C and the high C (including both these notes), we find that this interval encompasses eight staff degrees. Such an interval is called an *octave*.

50

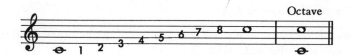

Octave

The repeated C's in the first measure of "The Swan" are called *unisons*.

Sing the song again and notice how the melody progresses in a descending step-wise fashion on "Do-de-ah-do." The intervals between each syllable are called *seconds* because they encompass only two staff degrees: C to B, B to A, and A to G. Examine the next two "do-de-ah-do" measures and observe that they are exact repetitions of the first one, only beginning on a lower tone. Such repetitions of a group of tones or motives are called *sequences*. Each of these motives encompasses an interval of a *fourth*: C to G, A to E, and F to C.

Fourths

In the context of the melody these fourths would be referred to as *descending* intervals, while the previous octave was an *ascending* interval.

Intervals similarly numbered may differ in the way they sound. For example, all seconds do not sound alike, a fact that is easily verified at the piano keyboard. Let us compare the intervals E to F and A to B, both seconds:

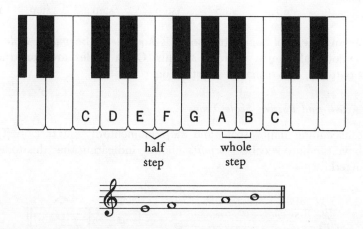

We see that there is a black key between A and B, but there is no key between E and F. Now, the distance from one key to its nearest neighbor, whether black or white key, is called a *half step* (minor second). Therefore, the distance between E and F is a half step whereas the distance between A and B is two half steps or a *whole step* (major second). Play these two intervals on the piano or bells and listen to the difference in quality between these two seconds.

The Major Scale Pattern

As you look at the piano keyboard, you will see that the notes for the C major scale coincide with the eight white keys from C to C:

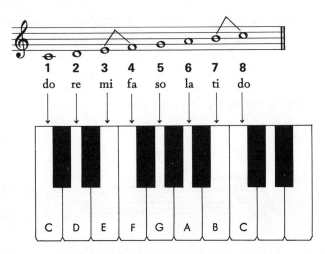

Examination of these keys reveals that the distance between them is as follows:

1		2		3		4		5		6		7		8
	whole step		whole step		half step		whole step		whole step		whole step		half step	

This arrangement of tones in a scale is known as the *major scale pattern* and all major scales must conform to this. Other scales are constructed on different patterns, as we shall see farther on.

Active and Passive Scale Tones

Sing the ascending major scale and stop momentarily on *ti* (7). The sign (⌢) above the note is called *fermata* (hold), indicating that this tone should be prolonged.

As you sustain this tone, you will notice that it has a strong tendency to want to move up to *do* (8) which, when sung, gives the impression of finality or repose to the ascending scale. *Do,* the tonic, is sometimes referred to as the "home-tone"; *ti*, the seventh degree, being only a half step away from the tonic has acquired a special name: *leading tone*, so called because of its strong tendency to move toward the home-tone.

Individual scale tones have different characteristics: some, like *ti*, are *active* (moving) tones; others, like *do*, are *passive* (restful) tones. The active scale tones are *re* (2), *fa* (4), *la* (6), and *ti* (7). The passive scale tones are *do* (1, 8), *mi* (3), and *so* (5). A feeling for individual tendencies of scale tones is a valuable aid to music reading.

Sing the following tonal groups quite slowly and sustain the tone under the fermata until you can "feel" what to sing next (up or down) in order to provide a satisfactory *resolution* for the *suspension* created by the prolonged tone.

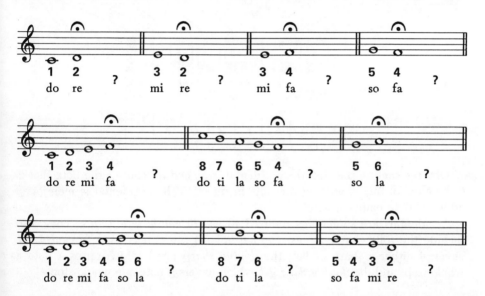

As you sang these tonal groups, you sensed that *re* (2) tends to move up to *mi* (3) or down to *do* (1); that *fa* (4) has a tendency to move down to *mi* (3) or up to *so* (5); and that *la* (6) seems to want to move down to *so* (5) or up to *ti* (7), which, in turn, would move up to *do* (8).

In summary: active scale tones have a tendency to move to the nearest passive tone. Becoming sensitive to this natural movement or tendency of scale tones is one of the many factors involved in developing note-reading skill.

ACCIDENTALS

The black keys on the piano also play a role in interval and scale construction. They derive their names from their adjacent white keys by the addition of *accidentals*. These are the sharp (♯) which raises the pitch of a note one half step and the *flat* (♭) which lowers the pitch of a note one half step. A sharp placed before F indicates that the next key to the right (a half step higher) should be played, and a flat placed before G indicates that the next key to the left (a half step lower) should be played. Thus, the black key situated between F and G may be referred to by two different names: F-sharp *or* G-flat. Similarly, all black keys have two names. The white keys B, F, and E may also be named in relation to their immediate neighbors one half step above or below by the use of accidentals. The following illustration shows how accidentals appear on the staff and where notes with sharps and flats may be found on the keyboard.

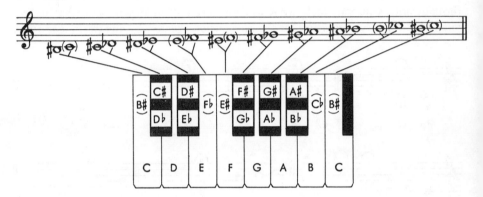

Observe that on the staff the accidental is placed *in front* of the note that is to be altered, but in naming the note in question the accidental is mentioned *after* the note name.

Accidentals are sometimes referred to as *chromatic alterations*. They also include the following symbols: the *natural* (♮) which is used to cancel the effect of either a sharp or flat; the *double sharp* (𝄪) which raises a note a whole step; and the *double flat* (𝄫) which lowers a note one whole step.

THE CHROMATIC SCALE

The C major scale is made up of whole and half steps and does not require any accidentals. This scale is called a *diatonic scale*. A scale which is made up entirely of half steps is called a *chromatic scale*. Chromatic scales may be notated in two different ways: with sharps or with flats. Sharps are usually used for the ascending scale and flats for the descending scale. You are already familiar with the syllables applied to the major scale. When accidentals appear in the notation, the syllables are altered as follows:

do	ti	te	la	le	so	se	fa	mi	me	re	rah	do
C	B	B♭	A	A♭	G	G♭	F	E	E♭	D	D♭	C

From this you can see that whenever a sharp occurs, the vowel changes to *i* (pronounced as *ee*) and that when a flat is used, the vowel changes to *e* (pronounced as in *day*) except for the syllable *re* which changes to *rah*. Sing this chromatic scale ascending and descending several times so that you are quite sure of the syllable alterations.

THE WHOLE-TONE SCALE

The whole-tone scale is a six-note scale, each step being one whole tone from the other. Compositions based on this scale reveal lack of any definite tonal center. The impressionist composers, Debussy, Ravel, Delius, and others liked to use it in their compositions (see Chapter 11).

WHOLE-TONE SCALE

TYPES OF INTERVALS[1]

Let us now consider various types of intervals that you should be familiar with.

Major-Scale Intervals

Intervals have general names which are determined by counting the lines and spaces including the two notes that form the interval. Examples:

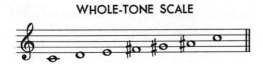

| unisons (primes) | 2nds | 3rds | 4ths | 5ths | 6ths | 7ths | octaves |

---

[1] Some instructors may wish to postpone study of the remainder of this chapter until Chapter 4 has been completed.

But, as we already have observed in the case of seconds, intervals of the same name may have different *qualities* (sounds) because they contain a different number of half steps. To describe these different qualities of intervals five terms are used: *Perfect, Major, Minor, Augmented,* and *Diminished.* After determining the general name of the interval by counting the lines and spaces, we can determine its quality as follows:

1. Consider the lowest note of the interval as *do* or 1 of a major scale.

2. When the upper note occurs in this scale, seconds, thirds, sixths, and sevenths are called *major* intervals; unisons (primes), fourths, fifths, and octaves are called *perfect* intervals.

Perfect	Major	Major	Perfect	Perfect	Major	Major	Perfect
Prime	2nd	3rd	4th	5th	6th	7th	Octave

3. Major intervals lowered one half step become *minor,* and perfect intervals lowered one half step become *diminished.*

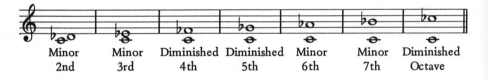

Minor	Minor	Diminished	Diminished	Minor	Minor	Diminished
2nd	3rd	4th	5th	6th	7th	Octave

4. Major and perfect intervals raised one half step become *augmented.*

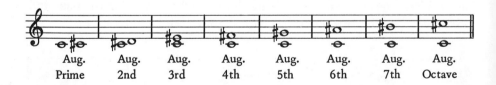

Aug.	Aug.	Aug.	Aug.	Aug.	Aug.	Aug.	Aug.
Prime	2nd	3rd	4th	5th	6th	7th	Octave

A knowledge of the basic intervals and the ability to recognize and hear them are very helpful in learning to read music and in part-singing.

Melodic and Harmonic Intervals

When the two tones of an interval are sounded one after the other, it is called a *melodic interval;* when the two tones are sounded together, it is called a *harmonic interval.* The two notes of harmonic intervals are usually written one above the other; however, primes and seconds are written with the notes placed next to each other.

Inversion of Intervals

The position of the tones of a harmonic interval may be exchanged. The bottom note may be moved up an octave or the top note may be moved down an octave. Such an exchange of positions is called an *inversion* and the interval is said to be *inverted.* The interval is inverted *upward* when the bottom note is placed an octave higher and it is inverted *downward* when the top note is placed an octave lower.

From this we can see that when intervals are inverted, perfect intervals remain perfect, major intervals become minor, and minor intervals become major.

57

Melodies are often harmonized by using parallel thirds and sixths. Here are two examples of songs arranged in this manner for two-part singing. The melody is in the upper part in both songs.

SAN SERENI

San Se - re - ni, de la bue - na, bue - na vi - da,

Ha - cen a - si, a - si los za - pa - te - ros. A

si, a - si, a - si, a - si me gus - ta a - mi.

AU CLAIR DE LA LUNE

Au clair de la lu - ne, Mon a - mi Pier - rot,

Prê - te - moi ta plu - me Pour é - crire un mot.

Ma chan - delle est mor - te, Je n'ai plus de feu;

Ou - vre - moi ta por - te Pour l'a - mour de Dieu.

INTERVALS AND CHORDS

Intervals play an important role in the building of chords. Chords may be made up of any number of tones in many different arrangements, but we shall concern ourselves here with only two kinds of chords, *triads* and *seventh chords*. You have been using both kinds of chords, the C and the G_7 chords, for accompaniments to the songs in the previous chapters, but without detailed knowledge or explanation of their construction. Let us now see how they are made up.

Triads

A triad is a three-tone chord and the familiar C chord is an example of a triad. When we examine this chord in detail, we discover that it is made up of two harmonic intervals sounded simultaneously:

As you can see, this triad can be described in two ways.[2] The preferred definition is that it is made up of a major third and a perfect fifth; or it may be said to consist of a major third and a minor third. The separate tones of the triad are designated as *root* (lowest tone), *third* (middle tone), and *fifth* (top tone).

Types of Triads

Triads may be built on any tone of a scale and are designated by letter names or Roman numerals according to their roots:

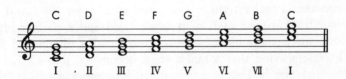

Notice that on the staff a triad involves three consecutive lines or spaces: *line-line-line* or *space-space-space*. This is an important visual concept to keep in mind when learning to read music.

[2] Remember that in analyzing intervals and triads we always begin with the lowest note and figure *up* from this note.

Play these triads on the piano and listen to the quality or sound of each. The I, IV, and V chords have the same kind of sound because they are all composed of the same type of intervals: a major third and a perfect fifth. Check this on the keyboard.

A triad composed of a major third and a perfect fifth is called a *major triad*.

The II, III, and VI chords also have the same quality but are different from that of the major triads because these triads contain a *minor* third and a perfect fifth.

A triad composed of a minor third and a perfect fifth is called a *minor triad*.

The VII chord is neither major nor minor. It is composed of a minor third and a diminished fifth and is therefore called a *diminished triad*.

To summarize: a major triad is composed of a major third and a perfect fifth; a minor triad is composed of a minor third and a perfect fifth; and a diminished triad is composed of a minor third and a diminished fifth. It is also worth remembering that a major triad becomes a minor triad when its third is lowered one half step; a minor triad becomes a major triad when its third is raised one half step; and a minor triad becomes a diminished triad when its fifth is lowered one half step.

60

Seventh Chords

The G_7 chord you have been using for your accompaniments is a four-note chord and, therefore, is not a triad, but a *seventh chord*. Seventh chords may be built on any note of the scale and the various chords, as with the triads, would have different qualities. However, a detailed discussion of these would have little practical value. On the other hand, the seventh chord built on the fifth degree of the scale, the V_7 chord (or *dominant seventh chord*), is used so frequently in song accompaniments that you should be very familiar with its construction.

The G_7 chord is built on the fifth degree of the C major scale; therefore, it is the V_7 chord in this key. Let us see how it is constructed:

As you can see it is made up of a major third, a perfect fifth, and a minor seventh. Another way of describing it is to say that it consists of a major triad with a minor third added.

The four tones of a seventh chord are designated *root, third, fifth,* and *seventh* and the chord is named a seventh chord because of the interval of a seventh added above the root.

Chord Inversions

All the chords we have discussed so far have been presented in root position, i.e., with the root at the bottom of the chord. However, the tones of a chord may be arranged in different ways without destroying its quality or aural identity.

A triad may assume three positions: *root, first inversion,* and *second inversion*. You are already familiar with the root positions of triads. When the third of the triad appears as the lowest note, the chord is in its first inversion; when the fifth appears as the lowest tone, the chord is in its second inversion.

61

Another way to identify chord positions is to observe the placement of the chord root:

> Root at the bottom—root position
>
> Root on top—first inversion
>
> Root in the middle—second inversion

Explore these positions of a triad at the keyboard.

A seventh chord may assume four positions: *root, first inversion, second inversion,* and *third inversion.* As in the case of a triad, a seventh chord is in its first inversion when the third appears as the lowest tone and in its second inversion when the fifth is the lowest tone. When the seventh appears as the lowest tone, it is in its third inversion.

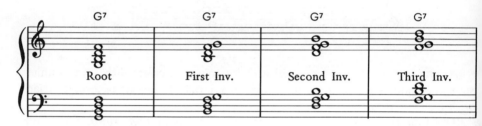

Note that the G_7 (V_7) chord you have been using for the song accompaniments has been the first inversion of this chord with the fifth (D) omitted.

Familiarity with triads and seventh chords, and their inversions, is a great help in learning to read music and in harmonizing melodies. (Harmonizing melodies is discussed in Chapter 7.) In learning to read music we distinguish between "scale-line" melodies (melodies which progress step-wise along a scale) and "chord-line" melodies (melodies which follow the outline of a chord as it progresses).

"Planting Cabbages" is a song with a melody that represents an even mixture of chord-line and scale-line tonal movement. Try to read this song "at sight" without the aid of an instrument.

PLANTING CABBAGES

Can you plant the cab-bage so, Just the same as we can do?

2. You can plant it with your feet . . .

3. You can plant it with your hands . . .

Here is a well-known melody, "Taps," which is based almost entirely on the second inversion of the C triad.

TAPS

Day is done, gone the sun from the lake, from the hills,

from the sky. Safe-ly rest, all is well, God is nigh.

Which part of the melody outlines the root position?

DEVELOPING SKILLS

Singing

1. Try singing "The Swan" as a four-part round.

2. Sing the two-part songs in this chapter and pay special attention to balance of parts.

3. Practice singing the following with letter and syllable names.

4. Practice singing the following chromatic sequences with syllables.

Playing

1. Play the above intervals and chromatic sequences on the bells and on the piano.

2. Find the C, F, and G triads on the piano (or build them with the Resonator Bells) and play them in root position and in inversions.

3. Play the melodies in this chapter on the bells.

Reading

1. Sing the following melodies with syllable, number, and letter names without the aid of an instrument.

(A)

(B)

(C)

(D)

2. Establish an appropriate beat; then clap or play each of the following eight-measure rhythm patterns. When these have been learned, perform them as *rounds*, one group beginning after the first group has sounded two measures. Also perform them as duets.

3. Name the following general intervals.

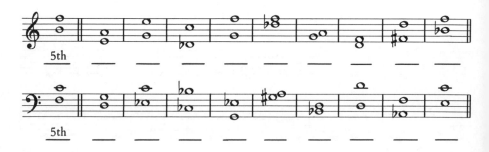

5th

5th

Writing

1. Complete writing the general intervals above the given tones.

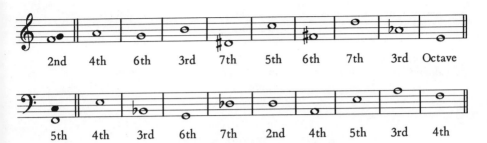

2nd   4th   6th   3rd   7th   5th   6th   7th   3rd Octave

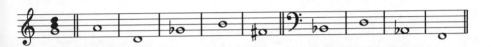

5th   4th   3rd   6th   7th   2nd   4th   5th   3rd   4th

2. Construct *major* triads on the following tones.

3. Construct *minor* triads on the following tones.

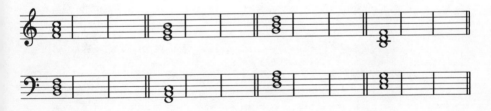

4. Write out the first and second inversions of these major and minor triads.

67

Define or explain the following musical terms:

active tone	half step	resolution
chord root	interval	sequence
chromatic scale	inversion	seventh chord
diatonic scale	leading tone	sharp (♯)
dominant seventh chord	major triad	suspension
fermata	minor triad	whole step
flat (♭)	passive tone	

ANALYTIC-CREATIVE ACTIVITIES

1. Play the C major chord on the piano and then find the C *minor* chord by lowering the middle finger one half step. What is the difference between these two chords?

2. Utilize your knowledge of the C minor chord to play the melody of "Go Tell Aunt Rhody" in minor. Why might this be appropriate?

3. Sing or play "San Sereni" in parallel sixths by adding a second part above the melody at the interval of a sixth.

4. Sing or play "Au Claire de la Lune" in parallel thirds by adding a second part above the melody at the interval of a third.

4

Major Scales and Chording

The songs studied thus far have all been in the key of C major. Although this is considered an easy key with which to begin playing such keyboard instruments as bells and piano, many songs are written in other keys in order to place them in suitable ranges for singing. Songs for children are usually pitched so that the melody can be written between middle C and E in the fourth space of the treble staff, this being the normal range for children's voices.

TRANSPOSING MELODIES

An example of a song written in the key of C that has a range too low for children's voices is "Bow Belinda."

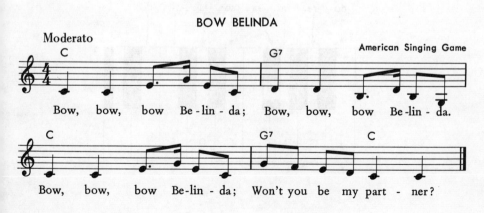

BOW BELINDA

Moderato

American Singing Game

Bow, bow, bow Be-lin - da; Bow, bow, bow Be-lin - da.

Bow, bow, bow Be-lin - da; Won't you be my part - ner?

When you sing this song as written, you will no doubt feel that it has been pitched too low for comfort. Let us see what it looks like in number notation:

$$1 \quad 1 \quad 3. \; 5\,3\,1 \; \big| \; 2 \quad 2 \qquad 7, \qquad 2\,7, \qquad 5, \; \big|$$

$$1 \quad 1 \quad 3. \; 5\,3\,1 \; \big| \; 5\,4 \; 3 \; 2 \; 1 \qquad 1 \; \big\|$$

The range problem occurs in the second measure where the melody goes down to G below middle C (5,). This and the preceding low B (7,) are also out of the range of the more common bell sets.

Now, instead of using middle C as the 1 (tonic), let us use the F in the first space of the treble staff as the beginning tone. As you sing the melody with the above numbers in this new key, you will sense that the whole song is higher in pitch and that the low tones you experienced in the key of C have been avoided. Shifting the melody from one key to another by changing the keynote is called *transposition*.

Play the melody on the piano or bells starting on F. Your ear will soon tell you that you must use the black key called B♭ to "make it sound right." To explain why this is necessary we must examine the major scale pattern once again. You will recall that the tones of the major scale were arranged in this manner (see p. 52):

1	2	3	4	5	6	7	8
do	*re*	*mi*	*fa*	*so*	*la*	*ti*	*do*
whole step	whole step	half step	whole step	whole step	whole step	half step

Let us see what a major scale constructed on F would look like:

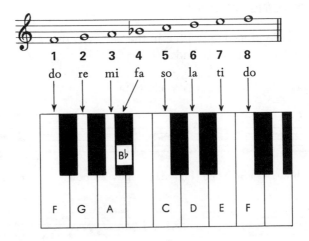

In applying the scale-pattern you find that you must play B♭

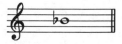

instead of B because there must be a half step between 3 and 4 (*mi* and *fa*). Confirm this with your ear by playing B and B♭ alternately. This, then, explains why you have to use the black key for 4 when playing "Bow Belinda" in the key of F. The notation of the song in this key looks like this:

BOW BELINDA

Instead of the *flat* (♭) being written every time it occurs in the melody, a *key signature* is used after the clef to indicate that all B's should be "flatted."

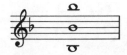

The key signature thus tells you which key you are in—in this case you are in the key of F.

If you were to play "Bow Belinda" on the bells or the piano beginning on G, instead of on F, you would have to use another black key, F♯, to make the melody sound right. The reason for this will become apparent if you build a scale on G according to the major scale-pattern:

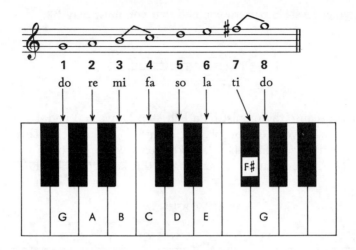

As you can see, in order to satisfy the requirements of a whole step between 6 (*la*) and 7 (*ti*), and the half step between 7 (*ti*) and 8 (*do*), you must play F♯ instead of F.

Since all F's must be "sharped" in the key of G, this is indicated by the key signature of "one sharp."

Transposed to the key of G, "Bow Belinda" has this notation:

BOW BELINDA

Bow, bow, bow Be-lin - da; Bow, bow, bow Be-lin - da.

Bow, bow, bow Be-lin - da; Won't you be my part - ner?

CHORDING WITH I AND V₇

You are already familiar with the I (tonic) and V_7 (dominant seventh) chords used to accompany the songs written in C major. You will recall that these chords were named according to their roots, the degrees of the scale upon which they were built. Thus, the C chord was called the I chord because it was built on the first degree of the scale of C, and the G_7 chord was referred to as the V_7 chord because it was built on the fifth degree of this scale (see p. 16).

In other keys the I and V_7 chords will have different names because they will be built on other tones. In the key of F major the respective chords would be F and C_7.

In the key of G major the I chord would be G and the V_7 chord would be D_7.

Chording on the Autoharp

To create accompaniments with the Autoharp for "Bow Belinda" transposed to the new keys locate the buttons marked "F" and "C_7" for the key of F and the buttons marked "G" and "D_7" for the key of G. Practice singing and accompanying this song in both keys. The number of strokes used in each measure will depend on the tempo in which you sing the song. Experiment with one, two, or four strokes in each measure. Which best suits the spirit of the song?

With these new keys and chords at your disposal you can enlarge your song repertory significantly. In singing and accompanying the following songs, use this procedure:

1. Establish the beat in an appropriate tempo.
2. Sing the song while conducting the beat.
3. Make up an accompaniment with the proper chords as indicated in the score. Some songs will require a chord on the accented beats only; others may require chords on unaccented beats as well. When a rest occurs on an accented beat, it will require a chord to keep the rhythm of the beat going. An up-beat (anacrusis) does not require a chord (see "Polly Wolly Doodle" and "Down in the Valley").

When you become more accustomed to playing the Autoharp, you will realize that every song demands a style of accompaniment appropriate to itself. Quiet and soothing songs demand slow, relaxed strokes; lively and vigorous songs require fast, crisp strokes.

POLLY-WOLLY-DOODLE

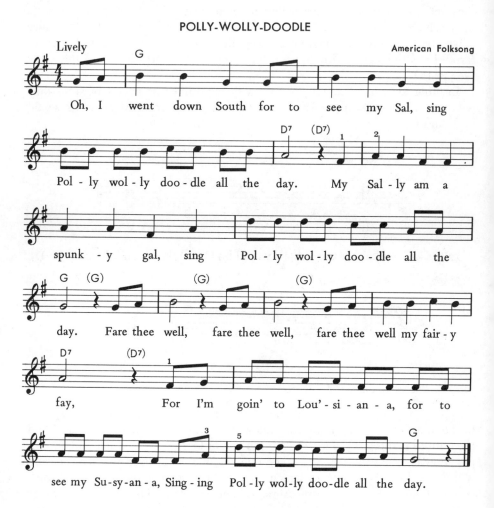

2. *Oh, my Sal she is a maiden fair,*
Sing Polly-wolly-doodle all the day;
With curling eyes and laughing hair,
Sing Polly-wolly-doodle all the day.

MARY AND MARTHA

Slowly

Spiritual

1. Mar - y and Mar - tha just gone a - long, Mar - y and Mar - tha just gone a - long, Mar - y and Mar - tha just gone a - long, Ring them gold - en bells, cry - ing, Free grace, un - dy - ing love, Free grace, un - dy - ing love, Free grace, un - dy - ing love, Ring them gold - en bells!

SHOO, FLY, DON'T BOTHER ME

Rhythmically

American Singing Game

Shoo, fly, don't both - er me, Shoo, fly, don't both - er me, Shoo, fly, don't both - er me, for I be - long to some - bo - dy. I feel, I feel, I feel, I feel like a morn - ing star, I feel, I feel, I feel, I feel, I feel like a morn - ing star. So,

D.C. al Fine [1]

[1] *D.C. al Fine,* from the beginning to *Fine,* the end.

DOWN IN THE VALLEY

Kentucky Folksong

Down in the val - ley, the val - ley so low,___ Hang your head

o - ver, hear the wind blow.___ Hear the wind blow, dear, hear the wind

blow,___ Hang your head o - ver, hear the wind blow.___

2. *Roses love sunshine, violets love dew,*
   Angels in heaven know I love you.
   Know I love you, dear, know I love you,
   Angels in heaven know I love you.

3. *Build me a castle forty feet high,*
   So I may see him as he rides by.
   As he rides by, dear, as he rides by,
   So I may see him as he rides by.

Chording on the Piano

When you were chording with the C and G_7 chords on the piano, you will recall that the hand stays in the same position for both chords and that changing from one chord to another only involves slight finger movements. Review the *fingerings* for these chords; in notation they are:

How these chords are fingered is of primary importance because, no matter what key we may transpose a song to, *this fingering for the I–V₇–I progression is always the same.*

Now try this fingering formula in the keys of F and G to prove to yourself that the fingering for the I and V_7 chords remains the same for *all* keys.

After practicing these chord changes, you will be ready to add piano accompaniments to your singing of all the songs in this chapter up to this point. Some of you will no doubt be able to play both the melody and the chords together.

Here are two songs with easy "five-finger" melodies written out in full piano score. Practice these with both hands in the keys indicated by the key signatures; then transpose them to the two other keys with which you now are familiar.

CRADLE SONG

LOVE SOMEBODY

CHORDING WITH I AND IV

Sing "Lovely Evening" in unison as expressively as you can, paying particular attention to voice quality and phrasing.

LOVELY EVENING

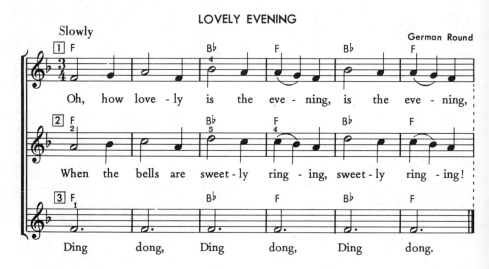

A new chord is needed to accompany this melody. This is the IV, or B♭ chord, which is built on the fourth degree of F major.

and

The fourth degree of the scale is called the subdominant, thus the IV chord is frequently referred to as the *subdominant chord.*

Chording with I and IV on the Autoharp

Find the buttons marked "F" and "B♭." Place the index finger of your left hand on the first button and the fourth finger on the second button. Practice the chord changes a few times and then make up a suitable accompaniment to "Lovely Evening," letting your ear tell you how many chords you should use in each measure to obtain the most expressive result.

Chording with I and IV at the Piano

To make the change from I to IV and back to I as easily and smoothly as possible at the piano we must rearrange the tones of the IV chord. In the key of F, the I chord (F) and the IV chord (B♭) have the following finger placements for left-hand chording:

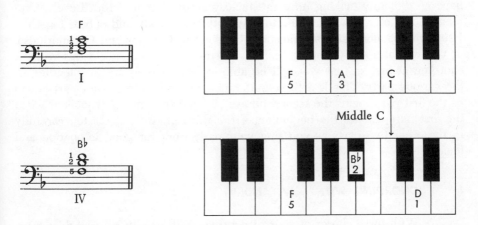

In making the change from I to IV the fifth finger (little finger) stays the same, the second finger (index finger) is placed a half step above the third finger, and the first finger (thumb) moves up one whole step.

79

In the right hand the chords look like this:

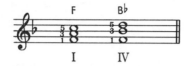

Study the fingering to make the change from one chord to the other.

Again, it is heartening to know that *these fingerings are applicable in all major keys*, making it relatively easy to transpose songs to other keys. Here is the notation for the I–IV–I chord progression in C major and G major:

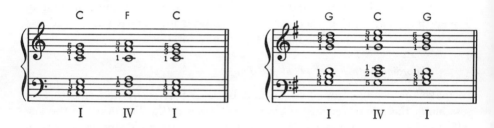

After a little practice with these chord changes on the piano, you should have no difficulty making up a satisfactory accompaniment for "Lovely Evening." Some of you will be able to play both the melody and chords together. Using chords alone at first, transpose the song to C major and G major, also.

You will also enjoy singing "Lovely Evening" as a round. Do this without chording at first so that you will be able to listen closely to the blending of the various parts. This is a three-part round in which the second part enters as the first part begins the second phrase (2) and the third part joins in when the first part reaches the beginning of the third phrase (3). Listen carefully to the other two parts as you sing your part; work for good intonation and tonal blend.

CHORDING WITH I, IV, AND V₇

With three chords at your disposal you will be able to provide accompaniments to many well-known songs. The four following are representative of the many types of songs that can be harmonized with the I, IV, and V₇ chords. We have limited ourselves to the keys C, F, and G because these are the only major keys available on the twelve-bar Autoharp. Songs in other keys are presented at the end of the chapter.

Chording with I, IV, and V₇ on the Autoharp

In singing and accompanying the songs, use the same procedure as before:

1. Establish the beat in an appropriate tempo.
2. Sing the song while conducting the beat.
3. Find the required chords on the Autoharp; remember the fingering positions for these: index finger on the I chord; middle finger on the V₇ chord; and fourth finger on the IV chord. Practice the chord changes I–IV–I–V₇–I until you can make them confidently.
4. Decide what style of chording is needed for the song at hand; then make up an appropriate accompaniment.

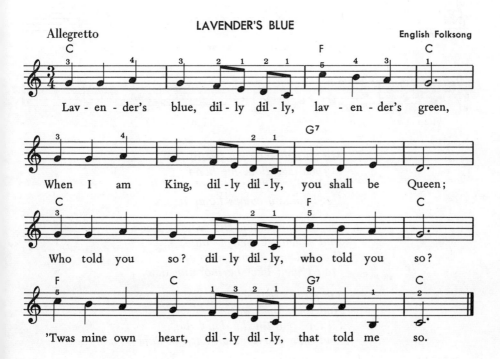

2. *Call up your men, dilly dilly, set them to work,*
   Some with a rake, dilly dilly, some with a fork;
   Some to make hay, dilly dilly, some to thresh corn,
   While you and I, dilly dilly, keep ourselves warm.

WHO WILL SHOE YOUR FOOT?

Appalachian Song

Oh, who will shoe your pret - ty foot,

And who will glove your hand,____

And who will kiss your ru - by red lips,

When I've gone to a for - eign land?____

2. *My pa will shoe my pretty foot,*
   My ma will glove my hand,
   And none will kiss my ruby red lips,
   Until Johnny comes home again.

3. *I'm sure you know the crow is black,*
   And sometimes purple-blue,
   If ever I prove false unto you,
   May I melt like the morning dew.

4. *Till all the seas run dry, my love,*
   And rocks melt in the sun,
   I'll love you till the day I die,
   And then you'll know that I'm done.

FOUR IN A BOAT

Appalachian Folksong

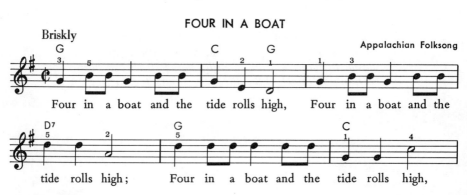

Four in a boat and the tide rolls high, Four in a boat and the

tide rolls high; Four in a boat and the tide rolls high,

Get you a pret-ty one bye and bye.

2. *Find your partner, stay all day,*
   We don't care what the old folks say.

3. *Eight in a boat and it won't go round,*
   Swing that pretty one you just found.

OH, NO, JOHN

English Folksong

On yon-der hill there stands a— crea-ture, Who she is I do not know. I'll go court her for her beau-ty; She must an-swer yes or no. Oh, no, John, no, John, no, John, no.

2. *Oh, madam, in your face is beauty!*
   On your lips red roses glow;
   Will you take me for a lover?
   Madam, answer yes or no.

3. *Oh, madam, I will give you jewels,*
   I will make you rich and free;
   I will give you silken dresses;
   Madam, will you marry me?

4. *Oh, madam, since you are so cruel,*
   And since you do scorn me so,
   If I may not be your lover,
   Madam, will you let me go?

5. *Then I will stay with you forever,*
   If you will not be unkind;
   Madam, I have vowed to love you,
   Would you have me change my mind?

In making up piano accompaniments for these songs follow the same procedure as for the Autoharp. The only difference is that you must be able to make the chord changes easily and accurately in order not to destroy the rhythmic flow of the melody. This is how the chord changes are made at the piano:

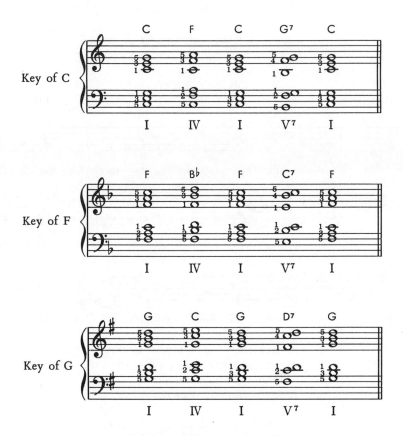

The following two songs, "A-Hunting We Will Go" and "When the Saints Go Marching In," written out in full score, are to help the novice piano player acquire skill in playing melodies and three-chord accompaniments simultaneously. They can also serve as exercises in transposition of melodies and accompaniments to other keys. Try transposing them to at least two other keys.

A-HUNTING WE WILL GO

Gaily

English Folksong

Oh a hunt-ing we will go, a hunt-ing we will go. We'll

catch a lit-tle fox and put him in a box and then will let him go.

WHEN THE SAINTS GO MARCHING IN

In march time

Song from New Orleans

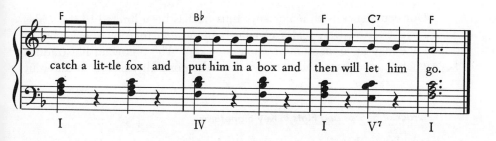

Oh, when the Saints_____ go march-ing in,_____

_____ Oh, when the Saints go march - ing in._____

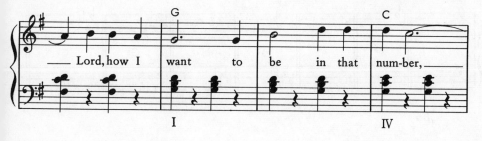

_____ Lord, how I want to be in that num-ber,_____

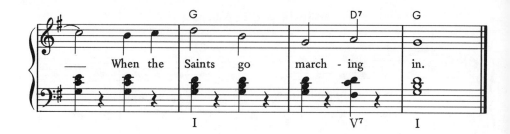

KEY SIGNATURES FOR MAJOR KEYS

Our experience with major keys thus far has been limited to the scales of C, F, and G. However, scales can be built on *any* tone on the keyboard and thus one may have many more choices of keys. The following illustrations of key signatures for sharp and flat keys show the possibility of fifteen different keys.

Order of Sharps and Flats in Key Signatures

You already know that C major has no key signature, that the key signature for F major contains one flat (B♭) and that the key signature for G major contains one sharp (F♯). Thus, the key having one more flat than C major has as its tonic a note which is four steps *above* C (F), and the key having one sharp more than C major has for its tonic the note which is five steps *above* C (G).

C major   F major   G major

In order to find the keynote (tonic) for the key having two flats in its signature, we must count up four steps from F to B♭; for the key having three flats in the signature, we must count up another four steps from B♭ to E♭; for keys with additional flats, we must proceed in the same manner. Therefore, the order of the flat keys, starting with one flat, is F, B♭, E♭, A♭, D♭, G♭, and C♭. The key signatures for these keys are notated as follows:

In order to find the keynote (tonic) for the key having two sharps in its signature, we must count up five steps from G to D; for the key having three sharps in the signature, another five steps from D to A; for keys having additional sharps, we must proceed in the same manner. Therefore, the order of the sharp keys, starting with one sharp, is G, D, A, E, B, F♯, and C♯. The key signatures for these keys are notated as follows:

Check these sequences of keys on the piano to make sure that you understand the order in which sharps and flats occur in the key signatures. In musical notation the sharps and flats must always appear on the staff in this order.

Finding the Keynote from the Signature

It is important to learn to identify the key in which a song is written by its key signature. This you can do very quickly if you remember the following:

1. The sharp farthest to the right in a key signature is scale-tone 7 (*ti*). Count up to 8 (*do*) or down to 1 (*do*). The letter name of 8 or 1 is the name for that key.
2. The flat farthest to the right in the key signature is scale-tone 4 (*fa*). Count up or down to find 8 or 1, the letter name of which is the name of that key. A shortcut for identifying the key from signatures having two or more flats is: "The next to the last flat on the right is the keynote."

Test your ability to identify keys from the signature by writing in the keynote for the following key signatures in the treble clef. Then write the keynote for the same keys in the bass clef.

PITCHING SONGS

To "pitch a song" is a common expression implying the establishment of the *tonality* (key feeling) and starting pitch (tone) of the melody. Songs usually begin and end on one of the tones of the tonic chord (I): 1–3–5 or *do–mi–so*.[2] Once the key in which the song is written has been ascertained from the key signature, the key feeling and beginning tone may be established in the following manner:

1. Sound the keynote, 1 or *do,* on a bell or piano.
2. Sing 1–3–5–3–1 or *do–mi–so–mi–do* to get the "feel" for the tonality.
3. Sing the initial pitch of the song.

For example:

When the song starts on *do*

do   do   mi   so   mi   do   do

When the song starts on *mi*

do   do   mi   so   mi   do   mi

When the song starts on *so*

do   do   mi   so   mi   do   so

Try your skill in establishing the key feeling and beginning tone with some of the songs in this and preceding chapters. After gaining experience in pitching the songs in the keys indicated by their key signatures, transpose some of them and then establish the beginning pitch from the new key signatures in the same manner.

---

[2] In minor keys the syllables would be *la–do–mi.* See Chapter 5, p. 110.

DEVELOPING SKILLS

Singing

1. Sing the songs with syllable and number names.

2. Practice the appropriate conducting patterns as you sing the songs with words.

3. Sing the following sequences many times in various keys.

4. Using your knowledge of how to "pitch" songs, find the starting tones for "Shoo, Fly, Don't Bother Me," "Down in the Valley," "Lavender's Blue," and "Who Will Shoe Your Foot?"

Playing

1. Play all the melodies on the bells and on the piano.

2. Practice playing several of the songs on the piano with accompaniment.

3. Develop facility in playing the I–IV–I–V₇–I chord sequence in the keys of C, G, and F on the Autoharp.

4. Be able to build and play a major chord, 1–3–5 (*do–mi–so*), on any white or black key on the piano. Then learn to play the I–IV–I–V₇–I sequence from any of these chords.

89

Reading

1. Establish the keynote and starting pitch and then sing the following melodies with syllable and number names without the aid of an instrument.

(A) Andante   Finland

(B) Allegretto   Germany

(C) Maestoso   Bach

(D) Allegro moderato   Denmark

2. Clap or play on percussion instruments the melody-rhythms of the above melodies.

Writing

1. Construct the major scales indicated by utilizing the major scale-pattern and then extract the key signature, as in the example given.

Example:

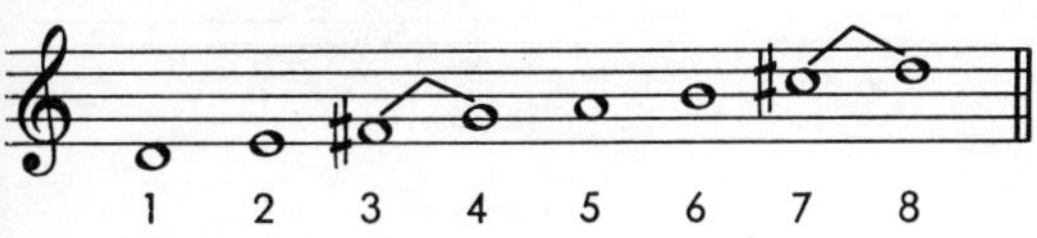

A major

B-flat major

E major

A-flat major

2. Notate the chord progression I–IV–I–V_7–I in left-hand playing position in the keys indicated by the key signatures given.

(A)

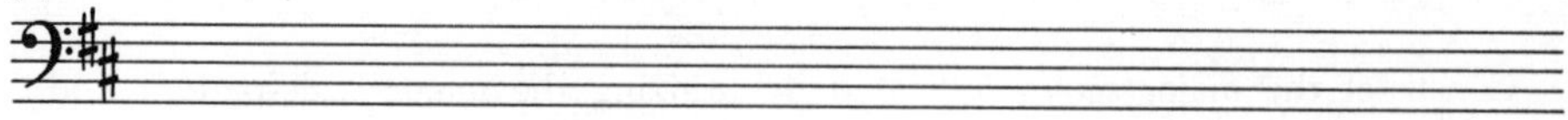

(B)

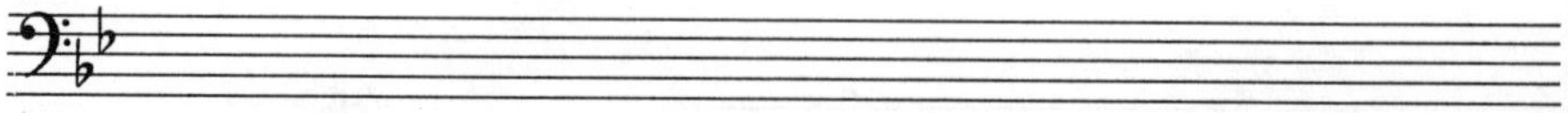

(C)

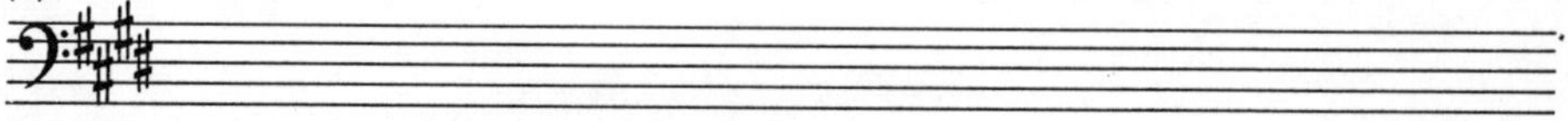

3. Transpose the first phrase of the following songs to the key indicated by the key signature.

LOVE SOMEBODY

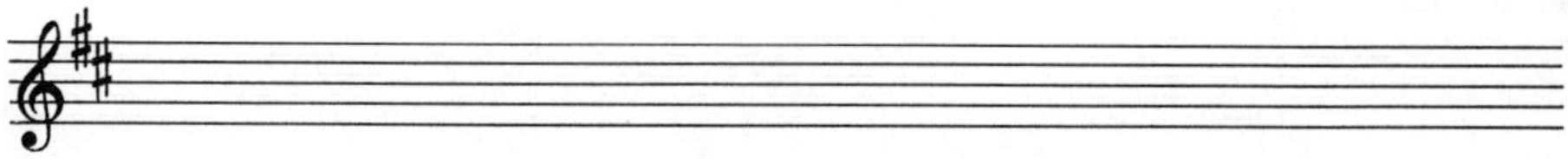

FOUR IN A BOAT

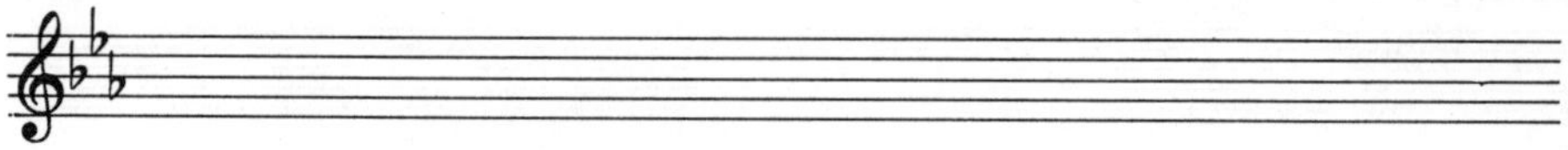

LOVELY EVENING

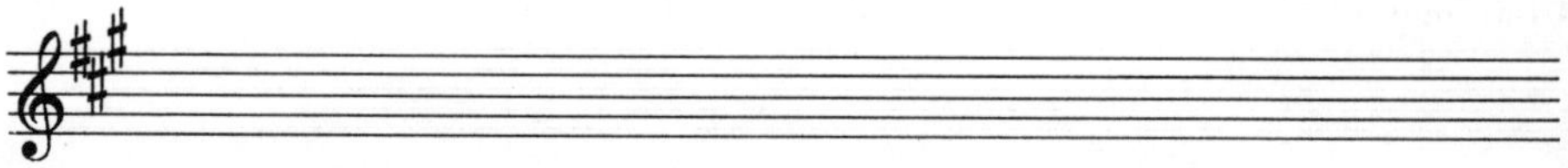

Vocabulary

Be able to define or explain the following:

D.C. al Fine
dominant
key signature
order of sharps and flats in key signature
subdominant
tonality
tonic
transposition

1. Transpose and play the following in the keys indicated.

WINTER ADE

Transpose to E, G, and B♭

OATS, PEAS, BEANS, AND BARLEY GROW

Transpose to D, F, and G

2. Create rhythmic rounds similar to those presented in Chapter 3 (p. 66) using various meters: $\frac{3}{4}$ $\frac{4}{4}$, and $\frac{6}{8}$.

3. Study the melody to "Cradle Song" (p. 35). Why is this an example of a three-part song form (ABA)? How is the phrase structure of this song different from that of "Lightly Row"?

4. Study the separate phrases of these two melodies. Can you discover any repeated tonal or rhythmic patterns within a given phrase? (Repeated melodic or rhythmic patterns are called *motives*.) Are any of these patterns repeated sequentially or with variations?

5. Using the knowledge derived from the above analysis, compose a melody in three-part form.

5

Minor Scales and Chording

Many of our favorite songs are in minor keys. The characteristic quality of the minor mode is evident in this Palestinian song of friendship:

SHALOM CHAVERIM

Moderato

Israeli Round

Sha - lom cha-ve-rim! Sha - lom cha-ve-rim! Sha - lom, sha - lom!
Fare - well, good friends, Fare - well, good friends, Fare - well, fare - well!

Le__ hit - ra - ot, le - hit - ra - ot, Sha - lom, sha - lom!
Till we meet a - gain, till we meet a - gain, Fare - well, fare - well!

* Pronounced: sha-lom khah-vay-reem

This beautiful song should be sung very expressively in legato style. Also sing it as a three-part round.

THE RELATIVE MINOR

From the key signature used for "Shalom Chaverim" you might have assumed that it was in F major, but your ear has already told you that this was not so. The explanation for this is that every minor scale shares a key signature with a major scale and begins on the sixth degree (*la*) of that scale. Major and minor keys which have the same key signature are said to be *relative*. Your concept of the key signature must now be broadened to include the fact that *for each key signature there are two related keys, one major and one minor*. Thus the key signature containing one flat (B♭) may indicate either F major or D minor.

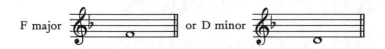

The following illustrates how these two keys are related:

Sing these two scales with syllables several times, starting alternately on *do* and on *la*. Also play them on the piano and on the bells.

The relative minor of a major scale may be determined by singing down to *la* (*do–ti–la*) which then becomes the home-tone of the minor scale. Here are two examples:

The relative minor of G major is E minor.

The relative minor of C major is A minor.

Check your understanding of this principle by finding these scales on the piano and by building them with the Resonator Bells. Also practice singing them with syllables.

Could you transpose "Shalom Chaverim" to E minor? What would happen if you transposed it to A minor?

Number Names for Minor Scales

In the above examples we have used only syllable names for the minor scale degrees because the same syllable names are used for relative major and minor keys. However, when number names are used for minor scales, the 6 (*la*) of the major scale becomes the 1 (*tonic*) of its relative minor scale:[1]

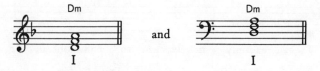

All chord designations in minor keys (I, IV, V₇, and others) are based upon this system of numbering the degrees of the minor scale, and we shall use it in what follows.

THE MINOR CHORD

Only one chord is needed to accompany "Shalom Chaverim." This is the chord marked "Dm" on the Autoharp. Find this chord, strum and listen to it a few times, and then proceed to make up an appropriate accompaniment for this song.

In notation, the D-minor chord looks like this:

and

Note that this chord is made up of the 1-3-5 of the minor scale. The chord root is 1 (D) and it is, therefore, the I chord of D minor. Compare this chord with the I chord in D major by playing them on the piano:

[1] Some teachers prefer to think of the minor scale as beginning on 6 (*la*) and they utilize the major scale numbers when they sing the minor scale. Their reasoning is that the syllable names do not change when one sings them in minor keys, thus neither should the number names change. However, when chord numbers are used, they must think of the minor scale as beginning on "1."

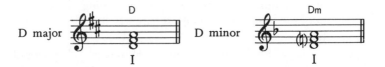

The D major chord becomes a D minor chord by lowering 3 one-half step. The same letter names, D–F–A, are used for both chords and the 1–3–5 arrangement is unchanged. D is the tonic in both keys, and the difference in the quality of the two chords is a result of the key signatures which make 3 in the minor key one-half step lower than it is in the major key.

On the piano the playing position for the I chord in D minor is the same as for D major.

"On My Journey Home" is another song in D minor, but it requires two chords, the I and IV chords, for the accompaniment. The IV chord becomes a minor chord in the minor key also.

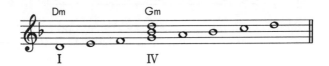

Find the "Dm" and "Gm" buttons on the Autoharp and place the index finger on the first chord and the middle finger on the second. As you practice alternating these chords, listen to the minor quality of this progression.

Use broad, relaxed strokes for your chording to this song; also try to preserve the long phrases as you sing the melody in a sustained legato style.

ON MY JOURNEY HOME

I feel like, I feel___ like I'm on my jour - ney home.

2. *Should earth against my soul engage,*
   And Satan's darts be hurled,
   Then I can smile at Satan's rage,
   And face a frowning world.

3. *Let all cares like a deluge come,*
   Let storms of sorrow fall,
   May I but safely reach my home,
   My God, my heaven, my all.

In playing the I–IV–I sequence in D minor on the piano, we arrange the chord tones in the same way as we did for D major:

THREE FORMS OF MINOR SCALES

In contrast to the major scale which is constructed on a single pattern of whole and half steps, there are three patterns of minor scales. These are the *natural,* the *harmonic,* and the *melodic* forms of the minor scale.

The Natural Minor

The two preceding songs were based on the natural form of the D minor scale. Let us compare this with the D major scale:

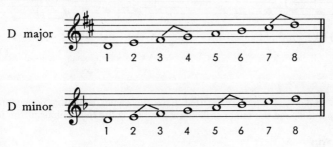

The difference between these two scales is in the arrangement of whole and half steps. In the major scale the half steps are between 3 and 4 and between 7 and 8, but in the natural minor the half steps occur between 2 and 3 and between 5 and 6. Play these scales on the piano and bells to make sure that you understand the difference between the two patterns.[2]

Review "Shalom Chaverim" and "On My Journey Home" and note that all the tones in these melodies belong to the natural form of the D minor scale.

The Harmonic Minor

Our next song is a familiar spiritual written in the key of D minor.

JOSHUA FOUGHT THE BATTLE OF JERICHO

---

[2] Major and minor scales that have the same beginning note (*tonic*) are called *parallel,* and the minor scale is referred to as the *tonic* minor of the major.

100

2. *Right up to the walls of Jericho,*
   They marched with spear in hand,
   "Go blow them ram horns," Joshua cried,
   "Cause the battle is in my hand."

3. *Then the lamb, ram, sheep horns began to blow,*
   And the trumpets began to sound,
   Joshua told the children to shout that mornin',
   And the walls came tumblin' down.

As you sing this song and look at the notation, you will discover a C♯ over the second syllable of "Josh-ua." Since there is no sharp in the key signature, this accidental requires explanation. The reason for the C♯ is that the melody of this song is based on the *harmonic* form of the D minor scale, whereas the two previous songs in this key were based on the natural form. Let us compare the two forms of the D minor scale.

Note that the seventh tone (7) of the natural minor scale has been raised one-half step to change it into a harmonic minor. This creates an *interval* of a step and one-half between 6 and 7 (B♭ to C♯) and this is the chief characteristic of the harmonic form of the minor scale. Play both forms of this minor scale on the bells and piano several times to familiarize yourself with their distinctive qualities. Also practice singing them, both ascending and descending.

For the accompaniment to "Joshua Fought the Battle of Jericho," we need only two chords, the I and V₇ chords in D minor. You are already familiar with the I chord in this key and know that it is a minor chord. Let us see what the V₇ chord looks like in the harmonic form of D minor:

If you compare this chord with the V_7 chord in D major, you will discover that it is the same chord that you have been using in this major key.

This would also be the case for all dominant seventh chords in major and minor keys which have the same tonic (begin on the same note): *the V_7 chords would be the same in both keys.*

The "Dm" and "A_7" chords are easy enough to find on the Autoharp and you have already used both of these chords previously on the piano for your song accompaniments. Notated in playing position for the piano they would look like this:

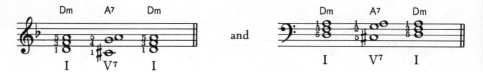

and

You will probably not experience any difficulty in making up an accompaniment to "Joshua Fought the Battle of Jericho" with the Autoharp. However, playing the melody *and* the accompaniment on the piano at the same time may cause some problems for the inexperienced pianist. Perhaps most of you will limit yourself to singing the melody and accompanying yourself with the chords indicated. An effective accompaniment can be created by playing the chord roots in the left hand and the treble-clef chords in the right hand, like this:[3]

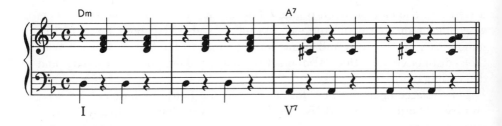

---

[3] See Chapter 8, "Variety in Piano Chording."

Our next song, "Go Down, Moses," is in the key of A minor.

GO DOWN, MOSES

Negro Spiritual

Slowly

	Am	E⁷	Am		E⁷	Am
1. When	Is - rael was in	E - gypt's land,	Let my peo - ple	go.
2. "Thus	said the Lord," bold Mo - ses said,	"Let my peo - ple	go.
3. "No	more shall they in bond-age toil;	Let my peo - ple	go.
4. "Your	foes shall not be - fore you stand;	Let my peo - ple	go.

Op - pressed so hard they could not stand, Let my peo - ple go.
If not I'll smite your first-born dead. Let my peo - ple go."
Let them come out with E-gypt's spoil; Let my peo - ple go."
And you'll pos-sess fair Ca-naan's land; Let my peo - ple go."

Refrain

Go down, Mo - ses, Way down in E-gypt's land,

Tell___ ole Pha - raoh, Let my peo - ple go.

Notice the G♯ on the word "people" every time it occurs. This tells us that the melody to this song is based on the harmonic form of the A minor scales:

1	2	3	4	5	6	7	8
la	ti	do	re	mi	fa	si	la

Three chords are required for the accompaniment: I, IV, and V₇ or "Am," "Dm" and "E₇."

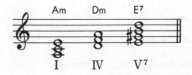

I   IV   V⁷

Find these chords on the Autoharp and make up an accompaniment appropriate to the mood of this song. Here are the same chords arranged for the piano:

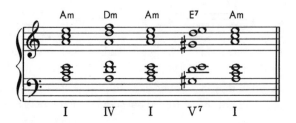

The Melodic Minor

The third form of the minor scale, the melodic minor, differs from the natural minor only in its *ascending* progression in which both 6 and 7 are raised one-half step. However, the *descending* melodic minor scale is identical with the natural minor.

Sing this scale several times as you play it on the piano or bells until you get the feel of the difference in the ascending and descending patterns. Can you sense any similarity between the ascending melodic minor and the ascending major scale starting on the same tonic?

The "Welsh Fishers' Song" is an example of a melody based on the melodic minor.

WELSH FISHERS' SONG

We know that be - low, un - der break- er and swell,

Lie the mag - i - cal caves where the sea fair - ies dwell.

2. *Far under the sea, where the green waters flow,*
   Fairies told the fish all the lore that they know.
   They fed those fine fish to a wonderful size,
   Come and buy them and eat them and learn to be wise.

For the accompaniment, you would use the same chords that you utilized for "Go Down Moses." For variety in piano chording, try one of the patterns suggested for $\frac{3}{4}$ meter in Chapter 8 (p. 133).

In conclusion, the three forms of the minor scale have one common characteristic: the half step between scale tones 2 and 3. The differences between the three forms are these:

1. The natural minor contains no accidentals.
2. The harmonic minor has a raised seventh degree.
3. The melodic minor has raised sixth and seventh degrees ascending; it is the same as the natural minor descending.

MIXING MINORS AND MAJORS

"When Johnny Comes Marching Home" is a lively song in the minor mode. It is also an interesting example of how a composer may use two forms of the minor scale, the natural and the harmonic, in the same piece of music.

WHEN JOHNNY COMES MARCHING HOME

Louis Lambert
(Patrick Gilmore)

When John-ny comes march - ing home a - gain, Hur - rah!___ Hur-

- rah!___ We'll give him a hear - ty wel - come then, Hur-

- rah!___ Hur - rah!___ The__ men will cheer,__ the

boys will shout, The la - dies, they__ will all turn out, And we'll

all feel gay when John-ny comes march - ing home.___

This song is in A minor. Observe the G ♮ in the third and fourth measures which occurs in the natural form of this key, while the G♯ in the next to the last measure is a characteristic of the harmonic form of A minor.

For the accompaniment you will need three chords: "Am" (I), "C" (III), and "E₇" (V₇). The III chord ("C") is built on the third degree of the natural form of A minor:

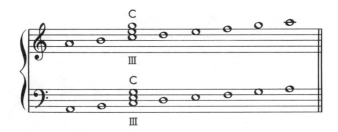

The chord positions below are the most convenient ones for the hands, but you may find the III chord sounds more satisfactory when used in the root position than the way it is notated here.

After you have reviewed the required chords, proceed to make up an accompaniment on the Autoharp. You will find that a rapid, crisp stroke will add rhythmic vitality to the singing of this song.

If you have the requisite pianistic facility, you may be able to play both melody and chords together. If not, use the following accompaniment for your singing (see Chapter 8 for other possibilities).

"The Erie Canal" has a melody that alternates between D minor and F major. The melody begins in D minor, changes to F major in the third phrase, returns to D minor in the fourth phrase, and then changes to F major for the refrain. Such key changes are called *modulations,* and this melody modulates back and forth between D minor and F major.

For the accompaniment to "The Erie Canal" you will need the I–IV–V₇ chords in both F major ("F," "B♭," "C₇") and D minor ("Dm," "Gm," "A₇"). Find these chords on the piano and on the Autoharp and review the chord changes in each key. As you proceed to make up the accompaniment, observe that the last chord ("A₇") in the third phrase over the word "hay" belongs to D minor, not to F major. A chord used in this manner in changing from one key to another is called a *modulating* chord. The last chord in the fourth phrase, the "C₇" over the fermata, serves as a modulating chord from D minor to F major. To help you with the piano accompaniment to this song we have notated it in full score.

THE ERIE CANAL

The simplest way to think about key signatures for minor keys is to relate them to the signatures for major keys. In Chapter 4 (p. 86) we provided charts showing in which order sharps and flats occur in major key signatures and we also explained how the keynote (tonic) could be determined from any given signature. You should review this part of the chapter at this point since complete familiarity with major key signatures is essential to determining key signatures for minor keys.

At the beginning of this chapter (p. 96) you learned that for each key signature there are two related keys, one major and one minor. Subsequently, you learned that every minor scale begins on the sixth degree (6) of some major scale. This gives you the cue for finding the keynote of a minor key from a given key signature:

1. Determine which major key the signature signifies.
2. Count up or down to the sixth degree of this scale (6). This is the tonic (keynote) of the minor key with the same key signature.

To test your understanding of this, notate the keynote for the minor keys indicated by the following signatures:

Major or Minor?

You cannot decide whether a melody is in major or minor from the key signature alone. You must also examine the melody itself.

In Chapter 4 (p. 88) you learned that melodies in major keys usually begin and end on one of the tones of the tonic chord (I). This is also the case with melodies in minor keys. Consequently, one must look at the beginning note and/or the final note of a melody to determine whether it is in major or minor. If these tones belong to the:

do - mi - so chord, the melody will be in major;

la - do - mi chord, the melody will be in minor.

If you examine the songs in this chapter, you will see that they all begin on either so or la and that they all end on la.

To confirm your understanding of this, indicate which keys the following beginning and ending pitches of melodies signify:

Key: _____   _____   _____   _____   _____

Finally, as you come to the end of this chapter pertaining to minor scales and chording, review the following principles pertaining to major and minor scales at the keyboard:

1. Major and minor scales having the same key signature are *relative*.
2. Major and minor scales starting on the same tone are *tonic* or *parallel*.
3. Every minor scale begins on the sixth degree of some major scale.
4. The dominant seventh chord (V_7) is the same in both major and minor keys of the same name.

DEVELOPING SKILLS

Singing

1. Sing the melodies with syllable and number names.

2. Practice the appropriate conducting patterns as you sing the songs with words.

3. Sing first the major scale and then its relative *natural* minor with syllables and numbers on D, E♭, F, and G.

4. Sing the natural, harmonic, and melodic forms of the minor scale with syllable and number names starting on B, C, and E.

5. Using your knowledge of how to "pitch" songs in minor keys (see p. 88), practice finding the starting tone for "Go Down Moses," "Welsh Fishers' Song," and "Johnnie Comes Marching Home."

6. Sing the following sequences many times in the keys of E minor, D minor, C minor, and F minor.

| 1 | 3 | 5 | 3 | 7 | 4 | 5 | 4 | 1 | 3 | 5 | 3 | 1 |
| la | do | mi | do | si | re | mi | re | la | do | mi | do | la |

I				IV				I					
1	3	5	3	1	4	6	4	1	3	5	3	1	
la	do	mi	do	la	re	fa	re	la	do	mi	do	la	

I				IV				V7				I					
1	3	5	3	1	4	6	4	7	4	5	4	1	3	5	3	1
la	do	mi	do	la	re	fa	re	si	re	mi	re	la	do	mi	do	la

Playing

1. Play all the melodies on the bells and on the piano.

2. Develop facility in playing the I–IV–I–V₇–I chord progression in the keys of A minor and D minor on the Autoharp.

3. Be able to build and play a minor chord, 1–3–5 (*la–do–mi*), on any white or black key on the piano. Then learn to play the I–IV–I–V₇–I chord progression from any of these chords.

4. Practice chording the songs on the Autoharp and piano to accompany your singing.

5. Practice playing several of the songs on the piano with the chord accompaniment.

Reading

1. Find the keytone and starting pitch from the key signature and then sing the following melodies with syllable and number names without the aid of an instrument.

(A)   Andantino   Denmark

113

2. Establish a firm beat; then clap or play on percussion instruments the following melody-rhythms taken from songs in this chapter. Can you identify the songs from which they were extracted?

Writing

1. Write the minor scales indicated by the key signature. Show both ascending and descending forms of the melodic minor.

Example:

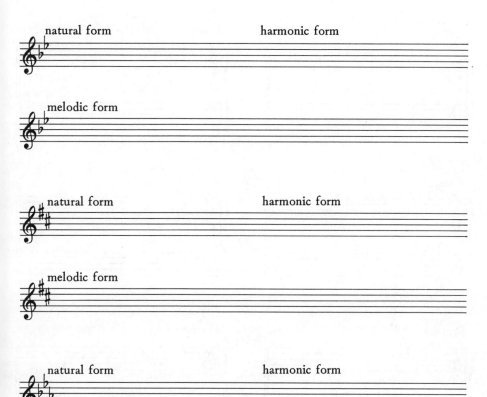

natural form   harmonic form

melodic form

natural form   harmonic form

melodic form

natural form   harmonic form

melodic form

2. Notate the I–VI–I–V₇–I chord progression in major and minor keys having the *same tonic,* as in the example. Write in the proper key signatures for the keys indicated.

Example:

C major   C minor

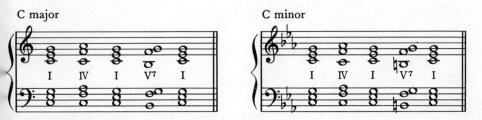

F major

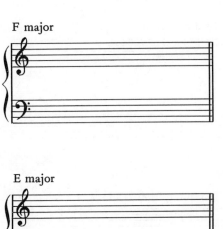

F minor

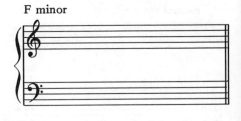

E major

E minor

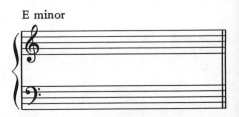

G major

G minor

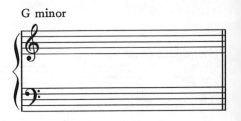

Vocabulary

Be able to explain the following terms:

harmonic minor
modulation
natural minor

parallel minor
relative minor
tonic minor

1. Transpose "Zum Gali Gali" to E minor and sing it in this key.

ZUM GALI GALI

[1] Pronounce: *he* like hay; *ch* as in German "ach"; *a* as in father; *u* as in rule; *le* with very short e; *o* as in come; *i* as in machine.

An approximate translation of the various Hebrew phrases: 1. & 2. The pioneer's purpose is labor; 3. The pioneer is for his girl; 4. Peace for all the nations. A suggested English verse is "We will work till daylight is done; We will fight till freedom is won." The words "Zum gali gali" are probably meaningless.

2. *Avodah le 'man hechalutz*
   Hechalutz le man avodah.

3. *Hechalutz le man hab'tulah;*
   Hab'tulah le 'man hechalutz.

4. *Hashalom le 'man ha'amim;*
   Ha'amim le 'man hashalom.

2. Compose a two-phrase melody based on the harmonic form of a minor scale. Harmonize the melody with the proper chords.

6

The Pentatonic Scale and the Modes

Our musical experiences thus far have been focused on melodies based on the major and minor scales. We shall now explore other scales and some of the music resulting from their use.

THE PENTATONIC SCALE

The term "scale" means "ladder" and denotes a series of rising pitches. One of the most interesting scales is the *pentatonic* or five-tone scale. It is considered to be important historically as the prototype of all scales, and it is found all over the world.

Theoretically, there exists a variety of pentatonic scales, but the one most frequently encountered in our culture may be notated as follows:

Note that this scale contains no half steps and that the pattern for it is:

1	2	3	4	5	(1)
whole step	whole step	1½ steps	whole step	1½ steps	

Play it on the bells or piano ascending and descending. Compare it to the major scale with C as the tonic. In what ways do they sound "different"?

Syllables for Pentatonic Scales

When syllables are used, they are related to the key in which the melody is notated. Thus, the syllables for the above scale would be: *do, re, mi, so, la,* (*do*). You probably used these when you were studying "Li'l 'Liza Jane" (p. 42) which is a pentatonic tune. Review this song and note that it utilizes only the five tones of the pentatonic scale starting on C.

"Old Texas" is another familiar song which is based on the pentatonic scale. As notated here the tonic is F.[1]

do   re   mi   so   la   (do)

OLD TEXAS

I'm goin' to leave___ old Tex-as now,___ They've got no use___ for the long horn cow,__They've plowed and fenced__ my cat-tle range,___ and the peo-ple there___ are__ all so strange. ___

---

[1] Key signatures are usually included when notating pentatonic melodies.

Pentatonic tunes may begin on any one of the five notes and thus one could have five different forms of the pentatonic scale. "The Riddle Song" exemplifies the following form:

so   la   do   re   mi   (so)

Note that the tonic is G but that the melody begins and ends on D, or *so*.

THE RIDDLE SONG

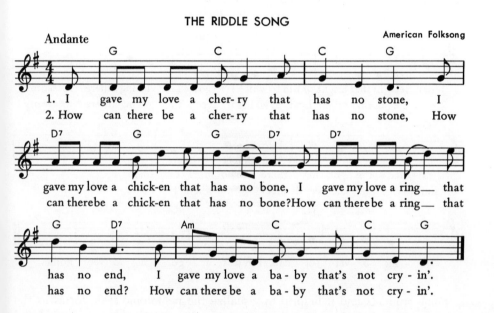

3. *A cherry when it's blooming, it has no stone,*
    A chicken when it's peepin', it has no bone,
    A ring when it's a rollin', it has no end,
    A baby when it's sleepin', is not cryin'.

A third form of the pentatonic scale is suggestive of the minor tonality. "Wayfaring Stranger" is based on this form which may be notated as follows:

la do re mi so (la)

WAYFARING STRANGER

Moderately Slow
American Folk Ballad

I'm just a poor way - far - ing stran - ger A trav - 'ling

thro' this world of woe, But there's no sick - ness, toil, nor

1. dan - ger in that bright world to which I go; I'm go - ing there to see my
2. trou - ble in that bright land to which I go; I'm go - ing there to see my

fa - ther, I'm go - ing there no more to roam,
moth-er, She said she'd meet me when I come, I'm just a

go - ing o - ver Jor - dan, I'm just a - go - ing o -ver home.

Some students find it helpful to visualize the pentatonic scale forms as the black keys on the piano. The three forms we have studied would be notated as follows for the black keys:

Can you transpose the three pentatonic tunes to the black keys?

THE MODES

When the term *mode* is used today in relation to scales, it is most likely to refer to those six that evolved through Hebrew, Greek, and Roman usage to become known eventually as the following: Ionian, Dorian, Phrygian, Lydian, Mixolydian, and Aeolian. They were used in the liturgical chants of certain religious groups, primarily the Roman Catholic Church. The Ionian modes is the major scale, and the Aeolian mode is the natural form of the minor scale. Thus, it is the remaining four modes which are "different." Examine them to discover their distinguishing characteristics. Note that the Mixolydian mode has a "flat 7" when compared with the Ionian (major) mode, and that the Dorian mode differs from the Aeolian (minor) only in that it has a "sharp 6."

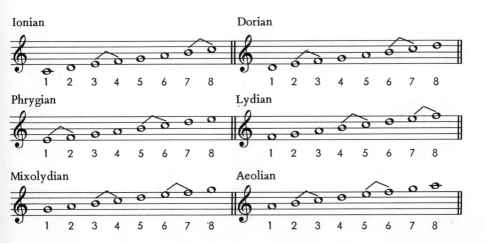

A great number of American folk songs are found to be modal. Spirituals and "blues" songs are frequently based on the Mixolydian mode. "This Train" is one such song. In the notation the mode has been transposed down one step:

THIS TRAIN

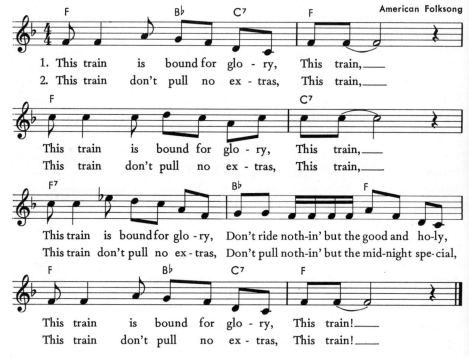

American Folksong

1. This train is bound for glo - ry, This train,____
2. This train don't pull no ex - tras, This train,____

This train is bound for glo - ry, This train,____
This train don't pull no ex - tras, This train,____

This train is bound for glo - ry, Don't ride noth-in' but the good and ho - ly,
This train don't pull no ex - tras, Don't pull noth-in' but the mid-night spe - cial,

This train is bound for glo - ry, This train!____
This train don't pull no ex - tras, This train!____

"The Shanty Boys in the Pine" is in the Dorian mode.[2]

THE SHANTY BOYS IN THE PINE

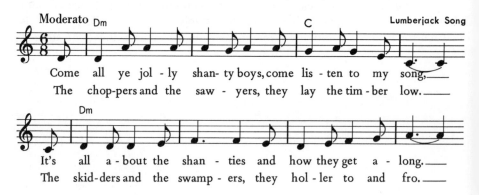

Moderato

Lumberjack Song

Come all ye jol - ly shan- ty boys, come lis - ten to my song,____
The chop-pers and the saw - yers, they lay the tim - ber low.____

It's all a - bout the shan - ties and how they get a - long.____
The skid-ders and the swamp - ers, they hol - ler to and fro.____

2 When singing this with syllables, start on *re*.

124

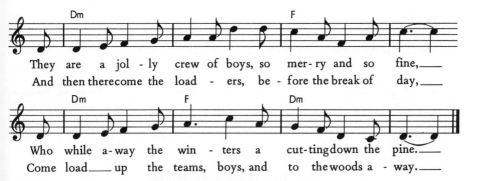

They are a jol - ly crew of boys, so mer- ry and so fine,____
And then there come the load - ers, be - fore the break of day,____

Who while a- way the win - ters a cut-ting down the pine.____
Come load____ up the teams, boys, and to the woods a - way.____

3. *The broken ice is floating, and sunny is the sky;*
   Three hundred big and strong men are wanted on the drive.
   With cant hooks and with jampikes these noble men do go,
   And risk their lives each springtime on some big stream you know.

DEVELOPING SKILLS

Singing

1. Practice singing the three forms of the pentatonic scale with syllables while making the appropriate hand signs. See p. 186.

2. Practice singing the modes with syllables. They may be grouped for comparison and sung in this manner:

Do modes: Ionian	....	d	r	m	f	s	l	t	d
Lydian	....	d	r	m	fi	s	l	t	d
Mixolydian	....	d	r	m	f	s	l	te	d
La modes: Aeolian	....	l	t	d	r	m	f	s	l
Phrygian	....	l	te	d	r	m	f	s	l
Dorian	....	l	t	d	r	m	fi	s	l
	(also	r	m	f	s	l	t	d	r)

3. Sing "Old Texas" as a two-part canon:

I'm goin' to leave ____ old_ Tex-as now, ____ They've got no

I'm goin' to leave ____ old_ Tex-as now,

Playing

1. Practice playing the three forms of the pentatonic scale starting on different tones. As you play them, identify the forms that relate to major and minor scales.

2. The following familiar songs are pentatonic: "Auld Lang Syne," "Old McDonald Had a Farm," "Get on Board Little Children," "Swing Low, Sweet Chariot," and "The Campbells Are Coming." Try to play these tunes on the black keys of the bells or piano.

ANALYTIC-CREATIVE ACTIVITIES

1. Using your knowledge of pentatonic scales and the modes, identify the scale or mode that the following songs are based upon.

EVERY NIGHT WHEN THE SUN GOES IN

American

Ev' - ry night _____ when the sun goes in, _____

Ev' -ry night _____ when the sun goes in, _____

Ev' - ry night _____ when the sun goes in, _____

I hang down my head _____ and mourn-ful cry. _____

YOUNG MAN WHO WOULDN'T HOE CORN

American Folksong

I'll sing you a song and it's not ver-y long,

It's a-bout a young man who would-n't hoe corn;

The rea-son why, I can't tell,

For this young man was al-ways well.

2. Create a short melody based on the tones C, D, E, G, A and notate it. Then create another tune of the same length in the same meter but with different melody rhythm and notate it. With the help of a classmate, play the two melodies simultaneously on bells, piano, or recorder. Evaluate the results. What conclusions can you come to about combining pentatonic tunes?

3. Select one of the modes other than the Ionian and Aeolian and compose a melody based upon it.

7

Harmonizing Songs

Your experiences in music will eventually lead you to songs for which no chord designations are provided, and you will want to be able to determine how to select the proper chords for the accompaniment to such songs.

CHOOSING CHORDS FOR SONGS

If you examine the chords used to accompany songs in major and minor keys in the previous chapters, you will discover the following general principles of melody harmonization:

1. The first and last chords in the song are nearly always the I chord. The next to the last chord is usually the V_7 chord and sometimes the IV chord.

2. The melody notes most often harmonized are those occurring on the accented beat or beats.[1]

3. The melody note that is sounded with the chord is usually present in the selected chord.[2] If more than one chord is available for this note, choose the one most satisfactory to the ear.

[1] In some songs it may be desirable to harmonize melody notes on other beats of the measure. See last measure of "The Erie Canal" (p. 108) and "Welsh Fishers' Song" (p. 104).

[2] Occasionally a chord will be played on a melody note that is foreign to the chord. See last measure of "A Cradle Hymn" (p. 30) and "Grandma Grunts" (p. 38).

4. Like phrases of the melody are usually harmonized with the same chords.

PROCEDURE FOR HARMONIZING SONGS

Whenever you find songs for which the chords are not designated, you can use the following procedure for harmonizing them:

1. Determine the key of the song from the key signature and the final note of the melody.

2. Make a chart of the chords that might be used in this key and of the notes contained in these chords.
   Example: Key of G major   I or G chord: G–B–D
                                 IV or C chord: C–E–G
                                 V_7 or D_7 chord: D–F♯–A–C

3. Decide which beat or beats of the measure you might like to chord.
   Examples: Songs in $\frac{2}{4}$, $\frac{3}{4}$, and $\frac{3}{8}$ meter are usually harmonized on the first beat of the measure.
   Songs in $\frac{4}{4}$ and $\frac{6}{8}$ meter are usually harmonized on the primary and secondary accents of each measure.

4. Choose a chord containing the melody note that is being harmonized and write the letter name and Roman numeral for this chord above and below, respectively, the melody note. (Sometimes a measure may contain several melody notes belonging to this chord.) You already know that the first and last chords of a song are likely to be the tonic chord (I).

5. If a melody note can be harmonized with more than one chord, write in the letter names and Roman numerals for these also; then choose the chord that sounds best to the ear when played in context with the preceding and following chords.

6. Look for like phrases in the song and use the same harmonization for these.

Analyze the chords that have been written out for "Twinkle, Twinkle, Little Star" with reference to the above six points. Check measures 3, 5, and 7 for possible choices of chords. What might these be? Are you satisfied with the chords chosen?

TWINKLE, TWINKLE LITTLE STAR

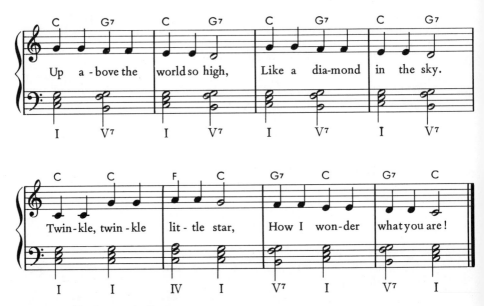

Nonharmonic Tones

All the tones in the melody of "Twinkle, Twinkle, Little Star" were present in the chords used for its harmonization. However, every tone of a melody does not have to be a chord tone and melody tones which are not chord tones are called *nonharmonic tones*. The melody to "London Bridge" exemplifies two kinds of nonharmonic tones: *neighboring tones* (*) and *passing tones* (+). A neighboring tone moves step-wise (up or down) from a chord tone and returns to the *same* tone. A passing tone moves step-wise between two *different* chord tones.

LONDON BRIDGE

There are no absolute rules of right and wrong to guide you in the harmonization of songs; any given melody may be harmonized in several ways depending on the extent of your knowledge of chords and on your musical discrimination. For the time being, your knowledge of chords is presumably limited to the chords you have been using thus far for songs in major and minor keys. But with these at your disposal, you can make up satisfactory accompaniments to many songs. Test your understanding of the procedure we have suggested for harmonizing songs by making up accompaniments for "Red River Valley," "Sandy Land," "Lullaby," and "Johnny Has Gone for a Soldier."

RED RIVER VALLEY

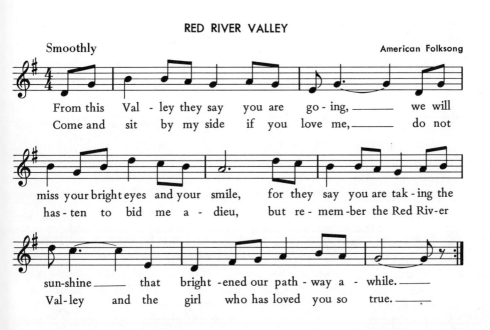

Smoothly   American Folksong

From this Val - ley they say you are go - ing, _____ we will
Come and sit by my side if you love me, _____ do not

miss your bright eyes and your smile, for they say you are tak - ing the
has - ten to bid me a - dieu, but re - mem - ber the Red Riv - er

sun-shine _____ that bright -ened our path - way a - while. _____
Val-ley and the girl who has loved you so true. _____

SANDY LAND

Lively   Play-Party Song

Make my liv-ing in sand - y land, Make my liv-ing in sand -y land,

Make my liv-ing in sand - y land, La - dies, fare you well.

LULLABY

Andante

Johannes Brahms

Lul-la - by and Good - night, with Ros - es be - dight,

With Lil - ies o'er spread is ba - by's wee bed;

Lay thee down now and rest, may thy slum - ber be blest,

Lay thee down now and rest, may thy slum - ber be blest.

JOHNNY HAS GONE FOR A SOLDIER

Andante

Civil War Song

1. There I sat on But-ter-milk Hill, Who could blame me
2. Me, oh, my, I loved him so, Broke my heart to

cry my fill; And ev - 'ry tear would turn a mill;
see him go, And on - ly time will heal my woe;

John - ny has gone for a sol - dier.
John - ny has gone for a sol - dier.

132

8

Variety in
Piano Chording

Thus far your piano accompaniments have probably consisted largely of "block" chords, i.e., the three chord tones struck together at one time. In this chapter we will suggest ways in which you may create other types of accompaniments. Besides providing a harmonic background for the singing and playing of songs, accompaniments are used to establish the tempo, the style, the mood, and the expressiveness of various types of songs. The possibilities for creating different types of accompaniments are almost unlimited. After you have explored those which follow, you will be able to invent others on your own.

There are two kinds of chording commonly used for piano accompaniments: left-hand chording to accompany the melody played in the right hand and chording with both hands as the melody is being sung or played on another instrument. Block chords may be used in either case; however, "broken" chords in which the notes of the chords are separated and played in succession offer many additional possibilities for variety in piano accompaniments.

LEFT-HAND CHORDING

To begin with, play "Little Duckling" with the familiar block chords indicated by the chord designations F, B♭, and C_7 (I, IV, and V_7).

LITTLE DUCKLINGS

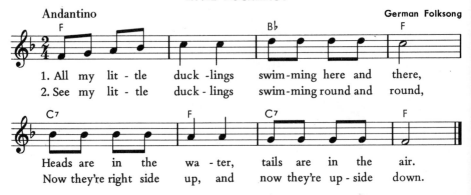

Andantino   German Folksong

1. All my lit - tle duck -lings swim-ming here and there,
2. See my lit - tle duck - lings swim-ming round and round,

Heads are in the wa - ter, tails are in the air.
Now they're right side up, and now they're up - side down.

After you are comfortable with this chording, try the three broken chord patterns which have been notated under part of the melody.

etc.

Such broken chord patterns can be used for a number of songs. Transposed to the key of C, the quarter-note pattern would be suitable for "Love Some-body" (p. 2), "Billy Boy" (p. 39), and "Grandma Grunts" (p. 38). The eighth-note patterns could be used for "Go Tell Aunt Rhody" (p. 3) and "Lightly Row" (p. 5).

Similar patterns can also be used in other meters. For songs in $\frac{4}{4}$ meter the chording could be one of the following:

134

Use these patterns, with the indicated chord changes, for your accompaniment to "Long, Long Ago."

LONG, LONG AGO

Andante

Thomas H. Bayly

Tell me the tales that to me were so dear, Long, long a - go,

Long, long a - go, Sing me the songs I de - light - ed to hear,

Long, long a - go, long a - go. Now you are come all my

grief is re - moved, Let me for-get that so long I have roved,

Let me be-lieve that you love as you loved Long, long a-go, long a - go.

In $\frac{3}{4}$ meter the accompaniment might be in one of the following patterns:

Try both of these patterns with "Oh, Where Has My Little Dog Gone?"

OH, WHERE HAS MY LITTLE DOG GONE?

Oh where, oh where has my lit - tle dog gone?

Oh where, oh where can he be? _____

With his tail cut short and his ears cut long,

Oh where, oh where can he be? _____

Transposed to the key of C, the same patterns would be suitable for "Susie, Little Susie" (p. 24) and "Lavender's Blue" (p. 81).

TWO-HANDED (RHYTHMIC) CHORDING

Another type of accompaniment that is very convenient and easy to learn is chording with both hands, leaving the melody to be sung or played on an instrument. The way this is done is to play the chord root on the accented beats with the left hand and the triad of the same chord, or one of its inversions, on the unaccented beats with the right hand.

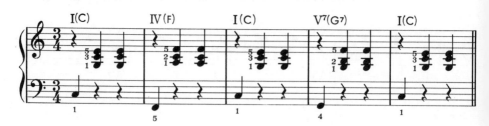

The advantage of this type of chording is that you do not need to be concerned about playing the melody. You do, however, need a functional knowledge of the triads and their inversions, and these should be reviewed at this time. See Chapter 3, page 59.

This kind of chording is sometimes called *rhythmic chording* and it is especially effective with many of our well-known American folk songs. The harmonizations of these songs are usually based on the I, IV, and V₇ chords, and "Old Smoky" is a very good example of this type of song. *Sing* the tune as you *chord* the accompaniment.

OLD SMOKY

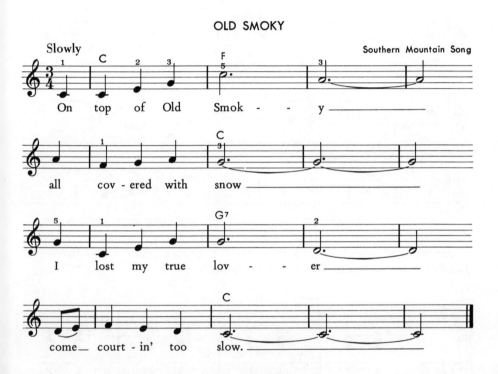

2. *A-courtin's a pleasure, a-flirtin's a grief,*
   A false-hearted lover is worse than a thief.

3. *A thief he will rob you, and take what you save,*
   But a false-hearted lover will send you to your grave.

4. *It's raining, it's hailing, the moon gives no light,*
   My horses can't travel this dark road tonight.

5. *I'll go up to Old Smoky, the mountain so high,*
   Where wild birds and turtle doves can hear my sad cry.

The same patterns, transposed to the key of G, are also suitable for "Sing Your Way Home."

SING YOUR WAY HOME

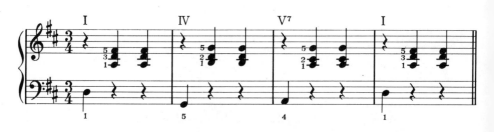

Sing your way home at the close of the day,

Sing your way home, drive the shad-ows a - way.

Smile ev - 'ry mile, for wher - ev - er you roam it will bright-en your

road, It will light - en your load, if you sing your way home.

An accompaniment of this type gives a proper lilt to "My Home's in Montana." In the key of D the chords would be:

MY HOME'S IN MONTANA

My home's in Mon - ta - na, I wear a ban - da - na,

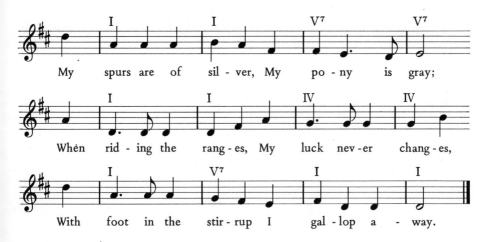

My spurs are of sil - ver, My po - ny is gray;

When rid - ing the rang - es, My luck nev - er chang - es,

With foot in the stir - rup I gal - lop a - way.

"Go In and Out the Window" is in $\frac{2}{4}$ meter and the chording pattern for this song could be one of these:

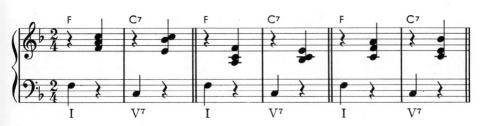

GO IN AND OUT THE WINDOW

Rhythmically

American Singing Game

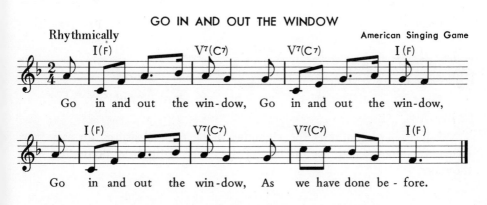

Go in and out the win - dow, Go in and out the win - dow,

Go in and out the win - dow, As we have done be - fore.

2. *Go forth and choose a partner (three times)*
   As we have done before.

Which inversion of the right-hand triad and seventh chord did you prefer? Why?

139

The same chords would be suitable for "Old Chisholm Trail" with the rhythmic pattern adjusted to the $\frac{4}{4}$ meter:

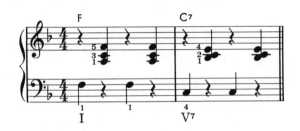

OLD CHISHOLM TRAIL

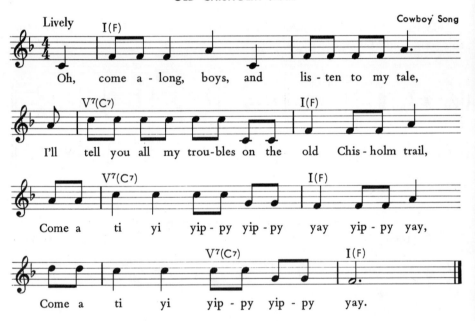

When a chord continues for a number of beats or measures, an easy way to avoid monotony is to use the fifth of the chord in the bass alternating with the root:

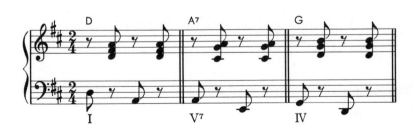

Try this pattern with "Camptown Races."

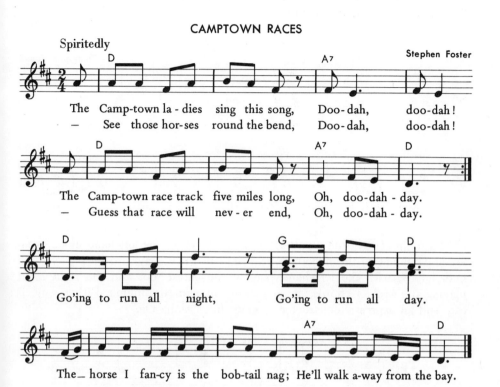

CAMPTOWN RACES

Spiritedly

Stephen Foster

The Camp-town la - dies sing this song, Doo- dah, doo-dah!
— See those hor-ses round the bend, Doo- dah, doo-dah!

The Camp-town race track five miles long, Oh, doo-dah - day.
— Guess that race will nev - er end, Oh, doo-dah - day.

Go'ing to run all night, Go'ing to run all day.

The— horse I fan-cy is the bob-tail nag; He'll walk a-way from the bay.

2. *The long-tailed filly and the big black horse, Doodah, doodah!*
   They fly the track and they both cut 'cross, Oh, doodahday.
   The blind horse stuck in a big mud hole, Doodah, doodah!
   Can't touch bottom with a ten-foot pole, Oh Doodahday!

3. *Old muley cow came on the track, Doodah, doodah!*
   The bob-tail flung her over his back, Oh, doodahday.
   Then fly along like a railroad car, Doodah, doodah!
   Running a race with a shooting star, Oh, doodahday!

This type of accompaniment can be very effective in minor keys as well. "Nobody Home" is in G minor and the chording pattern might be this:

Experiment with different inversions of the triad and seventh chord and find the ones that sound best to you.

NOBODY HOME

The following chording pattern may be played in the left hand alone as an accompaniment to the melody in the right hand. It may also be played with both hands, with the left hand playing the chord root and the right hand playing the broken chords, as an accompaniment for singing. Either way, it can lend an expressive character to songs like "Aloha Oe."

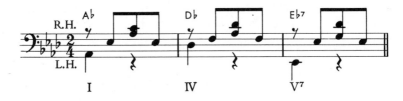

ALOHA OE

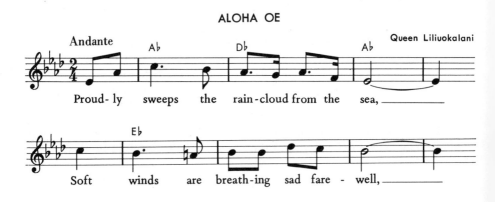

Tho' our part - ing brings such grief to me,

Mem'ries fond in my heart will ev - er dwell.

REFRAIN

Fare - well to thee, fare - well to thee,

The one I hold most dear of all my loved ones,

One fond em - brace be - fore we say good - bye,

Un - til we meet a - gain.

9

Composing Songs

Creative music activities in the classroom may take many forms and the composing of songs can be a motivating and highly satisfying musical experience. Furthermore, when one creates and notates his own songs, he demonstrates his ability to utilize musical knowledge. To this extent writing songs can also provide a functional review of many of the music fundamentals learned through singing, playing, and analyzing music.

CREATING A SONG

Among the approaches to creative song writing used in the elementary school are: (1) choosing a poem that appeals to the imagination and giving it a musical setting; (2) writing an original poem and composing a suitable melody for it.

Basically, there are four problems involved in composing a song:

1. Determining the rhythm and the meter of the words of the poem.
2. Translating the word-rhythm into line-notation.
3. Devising a melody that will express the meaning of the words or mood of the poem.
4. Notating the melody on the staff in a suitable key for singing.

144

Let us look into a fourth-grade classroom to see what is being done with this kind of musical activity. One of the students has made up the following little jingle:

"The human body is such a funny thing;
It has so many organs but they don't play a thing!"

The class enjoys these words and reads them in unison several times until everyone agrees that they are in the following rhythm:

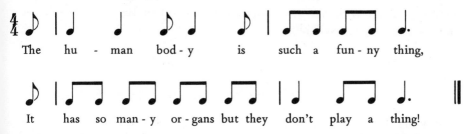

After establishing the rhythm of the words and translating that rhythm into note-values, all that remains is to put a tune to the words. Because this is a short verse, these fourth-graders, experienced in creating melodies, have little difficulty in deciding upon the following melody:

4	The	hu - man bo - dy is	such a fun - ny thing,
4	5	8 8 5 5 5	6 6 6 6 5

It	has so man - y or - gans but they	don't play a thing!
5	6 6 6 6 5 5 4 4	3 2 2 1

The teacher, who already has the words written on the chalkboard beneath the treble staff, has the task of deciding in which key to write this tune. Because the range of the melody is within one octave, she chooses the key of D major. This key places the song in a good singing range for the class. The song looked like this when it was completed:

THE HUMAN BODY

Fourth Grade

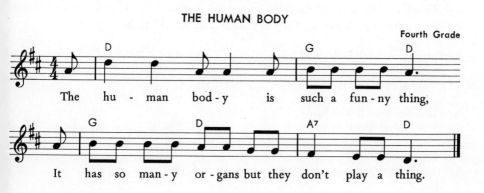

The children then copied the song into their notebooks so that they might have a permanent record of it for singing or playing at home or at some later time in school.

THE RHYTHM OF WORDS IN NOTATION

These children demonstrated that the first step in notating a song is to discover the rhythm and meter of the words. The procedure for this was to read the poem aloud as a rhythmic chant and to notate this in line-notation (see Chapter 1, p. 3) with bar lines inserted to the left of the most heavily accented words or word-syllables.

The | hu - man bod - y is | such a fun - ny thing

It | has so man - y or - gans but they | don't play a thing!

Deciding on the proper meter for the rhyme posed a problem because the meter of this jingle could be either duple or quadruple; however, the word-rhythm of the second line with the emphasis on the word "don't" seemed to indicate quadruple meter.

The line-notation was then translated into music notation with the quarter note as the beat unit shown above. Notice that the children sensed that this poem would call for a "pick-up" note at the beginning (♪) and that the note values of the last measure would have to "complement" this note to make up a full measure (♩ ♪♩♩.). Notice also that they placed the most important words or word-syllables on the accented beats and the less important words, such as "the," "it," and "a," on the unaccented beats.

Word Rhythms in Common Meters

In preparing to notate your own songs you may need practice in translating the rhythm of words into notation. The cheers used at athletic events are sometimes excellent word-rhythms to notate. Perhaps the best known of these is "We want a touchdown!" First we write the words, then:

1. Speak the words (to find line-notation and accents).

We want a touch-down! We want a

2. Place bar lines left of heavily accented words.

3. Translate into music notation.

146

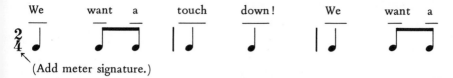

(Add meter signature.)

Using the above as an example, continue with the following words that we have selected to help you translate word-rhythms into notation. The first two are in duple or quadruple meter, $\frac{2}{4}$ or $\frac{4}{4}$. After you have worked with the first two examples, look at their notation in the book to be sure you are proceeding correctly.

1. Hush, my dear, lie still and slumber (p. 30).

2. Go tell Aunt Rho-dy the old gray goose is dead (p. 3).

3. Ding dong bell, — Pus-sy's in the well. —

4. Peas por-ridge hot; peas por-ridge cold,
   Peas por-ridge in the pot, nine days old. —

5. Baa baa black sheep, have you an-y wool? —
   Yes sir, yes sir, three bags full. —

A helpful hint is that unimportant words such as "a" and "the" are very rarely on accented beats of the measure. They are also ordinarily assigned to notes of relatively short duration. Important words are almost always on accented beats and have notes of longer value.

Next try to notate words in $\frac{3}{4}$ or $\frac{3}{8}$ meter. The first two examples are from songs in this book. First notate the word rhythms; then compare what you have written with the notation in the book.

1. Oh, how lovely is the evening (p. 78).

2. Sing your way home at the close of the day (p. 138).

3. Sweetly I sing to you under the moon.

4. We wish you a merry Christmas, we wish you a merry Christmas.

The following words should be notated in fast $\frac{6}{8}$ meter. Starting with the words you know in the first example will help you to identify the characteristic rhythmic patterns in this meter: and

1. Row, row, row your boat (p. 33).

2. Lit-tle Boy Blue, come blow your horn, — the
   Sheep's in the mead-ow, the cow's in the corn.

3. He's a jol-ly good fel-low, which no-bod-y can deny. —

147

STEPS IN COMPOSING SONGS

Now try to create and notate some songs of your own. This can be done by you alone or as a cooperative project by the class as described below. The best poems to begin with are those in which the words have a simple and direct rhythm such as:

Fog

The fog is rising slowly
Soon it will be high;
Then the gulls will soar again
Far up in the sky.

1. Write the words under the treble staff on the chalkboard or in a notebook. Discuss the meaning and mood of the poem and look for words that could suggest the rise or fall of the melody line.

2. Speak the words in unison until everyone feels the same word-rhythm. Your class might feel the rhythm of this poem to be either $\frac{2}{4}$ or $\frac{6}{8}$ meter.

3. Find and mark the most heavily accented words. (Clapping the word-rhythm and conducting the meter can help in steps 2 and 3.)

4. Place bar lines in front of the most heavily accented words or word-syllables. Remember that some poems require a "pick-up" note before the first bar line.

5. Find a melody for the first line. Several individuals can contribute their different melodies, and the class will decide which of them is best suited to the mood and thought of the words. Some class members might choose the Song Bells, piano, or other instruments as the medium by which they create their melodies.

6. Sing the chosen melody several times until everyone in the class can remember it.

7. Write the numbers, syllables, or letter names of the melody under the words.

8. Continue this process with the second line of the words. One way to do this is to sing the first line, then silently think the melody of the second line. Then repeat this; only this time, sing the second line.

9. Continue in the above manner to the end of the poem.

10. Translate the numbers or syllable names into notation. First, select the key you will use by placing the song in the best singing range according to its highest and lowest tones. Next, place the notes on the staff.

11. Harmonize the melody on the piano or Autoharp in accordance with the principles of harmonization that you learned in Chapter 7.

12. Make appropriate use of the tempo and expression marks you have learned in previous chapters of this book.

Try setting some of the following poems to music:

WINTER

Snow is falling silently,
The wind is standing still.
Birds are making little tracks
Upon the window sill.

MOONLIGHT

Dark is the night as I lie in my bed;
The stars and the moon give light.
As I lie in my bed, resting my head,
I go to sleep; I go to sleep.

THE SNOWMAN

I wish I were a snowman,
So fat and round and still;
Then I would watch the children,
Come sliding down the hill.

DEVELOPING SKILLS

1. Notate some of your favorite cheers used at athletic events.

2. Word-rhythms played on a drum have been called "drum-talk." Play on a drum, then notate such geographical names as Mississippi River; Portland, Oregon; and Birmingham, Alabama.

3. Compare "A Cradle Hymn" (p. 30) and "Cradle Song" (p. 77) to find out if you can explain why the first song is in $\frac{4}{4}$ meter and the second one is in $\frac{2}{4}$ meter.

4. Choose nursery rhymes and poems from other sources and set them to music.

5. Create your own poems and set them to music. (It is not always necessary for words to rhyme.)

6. Harmonize your songs, choosing a type of accompaniment suited to the mood of the poem.

7. Try to write down the original songs of classmates as they sing them. This will take practice.

10

Concepts of Musical Form

All works of art have form of some kind. Form in music is the way in which rhythm, melody, and harmony are put together to make a unified whole. You have already become familiar with some of the basic concepts of musical form: melodic movement and contour, phrases and cadences, rhythmic and melodic motives, repetition and sequence, two- and three-part forms. In this chapter we shall examine the formal aspects of music more fully and also extend our knowledge of musical form to include some of the larger forms of music through recorded examples of instrumental music.

PHRASE AND CADENCE

The phrase may be considered the basic unit of musical structure. It usually contains one or more melodic or rhythmic motives used in repetition or sequence. Cadences are musical punctuation marks or phrase endings. They may be conclusive (complete) or inconclusive (incomplete); the degree of finality is dependent upon rhythmic, melodic, or harmonic movement.

From a rhythmic standpoint, cadences usually occur on a note of long duration or on a relatively long note followed by a rest. Melodically, a cadence is considered complete when the phrase ends on the tonic and incomplete when it ends on any other tone. Harmonically, cadences are defined in terms of the chord progression that occurs at the end of the phrases. They are classified as follows:

150

Half cadence: phrase ending on V or V$_7$.

Authentic cadence: phrase ending on I preceded by V or V$_7$.

Plagal cadence: phrase ending on I preceded by IV.

Deceptive cadence: phrase ending on unexpected chord.

Phrase lengths of two, four, or eight measures may be considered the norm. However, phrases may vary greatly in length and in clarity, and it is not always easy to determine where one phrase ends and another begins.

PERIOD AND PHRASE GROUP

The period, sometimes called *sentence,* consists of two phrases having contrasting cadences. The first phrase, the *antecedent,* is usually terminated by a half cadence; the second, or *consequent* phrase, terminates with an authentic cadence. The period is said to be a complete musical statement.

The *double period* consists of four phrases having a half cadence in the middle and an authentic cadence at the end.

The *phrase group* is a unit of three or more phrases, sometimes of unequal length, the last of which ends with an authentic cadence.

The following songs exemplify the above phrase forms. Analyze the cadences to reinforce your understanding of these concepts.

Period

"Love Somebody"	p. 2
"He's Got the Whole World in His Hands"	p. 43
"Four in a Boat"	p. 82

Double Period

"Billy Boy"	p. 39
"Lavender's Blue"	p. 81
"When the Saints Go Marching In"	p. 85

Phrase Group

"Oh, No, John"	p. 83
"Sing Your Way Home"	p. 138

PART FORMS

In Chapter 1 the phrase structure of songs was examined and it was discovered that phrases may repeat exactly, that they may repeat with some variation, or that they may be different and thus contrasting. Phrases were found to be arranged in ways that resulted in two-part (*binary*) and three-part (*ternary*) forms. However, these forms tend to outgrow the simple phrase arrangements in more complex songs and in instrumental compositions. These may have a period, a double period, or a phrase group as one of the parts. Thus, the concept of what constitutes a particular part form must include a consideration of these possibilities. When analyzing the longer forms it is customary to designate the separate phrases by small letters (a, b, c, d, etc.) and to label the various parts with capital letters (A, AB). Note the variations in phrase arrangement of the following songs and that the immediate repetition of a phrase is not considered to add another part to the form.

Two-part Form (AB)		Phrase Arrangement	
"Li'l 'Liza Jane"	p. 42	(a, a)	(b, b)
"On My Journey Home"	p. 98	(a, a)	(b, b)
"Lullaby"	p. 132	(a, b)	(c, c)

Three-part Form (ABA)		Phrase Arrangement	
"Susie, Little Susie"	p. 24	(a, a)	b, a
"Cradle Song"	p. 35	a, b, a	
"Shoo, Fly, Don't Bother Me"	p. 75	(a, a) (b, b) (a, a)	

Binary and ternary forms are also encountered frequently in instrumental music. In some instances they will be very simple in structure, but at other times they may be more varied and complex. The recorded examples on the following pages illustrate different arrangements of binary and ternary structures.[1]

The binary form played an important role in the music written in the Baroque period (see Chapter 11). It was a highly stylized form and the material of the two parts, A and B, was closely related. The first part would modulate to a related key, closing with a cadence in this key. The second part would begin in the new key, then modulate back to the original (tonic) key. The B section would frequently be made up of material taken from the A section through simple repetition or a kind of development. It is often somewhat longer than the A section.

---

[1] The recorded instrumental compositions referred to in this book may be found in the following Educational Record Series:
    Adventures in Music (RCA–Victor)—AIM
    Bowmar Orchestral Library (Bowmar Records)—BOL

BADINERIE FROM SUITE NO. 2
IN B MINOR FOR FLUTE AND STRINGS·

Bach
AIM III-1

Additional examples of binary form:

Ginastera: "Wheat Dance" from *Estansia*	AIM	IV-1
Handel: Bourée and Menuetto from *Royal Fireworks Music*	AIM	III-2
	BOL	62
Milhaud: "Copacabana" from *Saudades do Brazil*	AIM	IV-2
Respighi: "Danza" from *Brazilian Impressions*	AIM	V-2

The basic scheme of the ternary form is *statement-departure-restatement* (ABA), but this may be enlarged and expanded by repetition of sections, introductions, interludes, and codas. The key to listening is to recognize the return of the first section (A).

TREPAK FROM " NUTCRACKER SUITE "

Tchaikovsky
BOL 58

Additional examples of ternary form:

Brahms: Hungarian Dance No. 1 in C Minor	AIM	V-2
Copland: Circus Music	AIM	III-1
Debussy: *En Bateau*	BOL	53
Offenbach: Barcarolle from *Tales of Hoffman*	AIM	III-1
Schumann: *Traumerei*	AIM	IV-2
	BOL	63
Stravinsky: Berceuse from *Firebird Suite*	AIM	I
Vaughan Williams: Fantasia on "Greensleeves"	AIM	VI-2
Walton: Waltz from *Façade* Suite	AIM	VI-2

153

The *compound ternary* form is an extended structure in which each part may be a simple binary or tenary form in itself. This form is used consistently in the classical minuets of Haydn and Mozart. The middle part (B) is called *Trio* and the outer parts are called *Minuet*. This form may be diagrammed as follows:

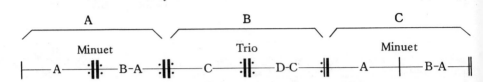

Note that when the minuet is restated, the two parts, A and B, are not repeated.

MINUET FROM SYMPHONY NO. 40 IN G MINOR

Mozart
BOL 62

Additional examples of compound ternary form:

Bizet: Minuetto from *L'Arlésienne* Suite No. 1	AIM	IV-2
Haydn: Menuetto from Symphony No. 6 in G Major	BOL	63
Mozart: Menuetto from Divertimento No. 17 in D	AIM	V-2
Sousa: March, "Stars and Stripes Forever"	AIM	IV-2
	BOL	60

RONDO FORM

The structural plan of the rondo is the alternation of a *principal* theme with one or more *subordinate* themes. The principal theme must occur at least three times. These restatements may be in the form of exact repetitions, or variants, or abbreviations. The subordinate themes present new materials and new key centers. Themes may vary in length from a single phrase to one of the part forms.

The rondo design may be expressed in formulas such as ABACA, ABACADA, and so on. As can be seen, the recurrence of "A" is the unique characteristic of the rondo form. The exact number of divisions in a rondo is not prescribed and the order of repetition of themes is frequently varied.

RONDEAU FROM SUITE NO. 2
IN B MINOR FOR FLUTE AND STRINGS

Additional examples of rondo form:

Beethoven: Scherzo from Symphony No. 7 in A Major	BOL	62
Dvořák: Slavonic Dance in C Minor	AIM	IV-2
Haydn: Gypsy Rondo from Trio in G Major	BOL	64
Khachaturian: Waltz from *Masquerade* Suite	AIM	IV-2
Mozart: Romanza from *Eine kleine Nachtmusik*	AIM	IV-1
Prokofieff: "Waltz on Ice" from *Winter Holiday*	AIM	III-2
Smetana: "Dance of the Comedians" from *Bartered Bride*	AIM	VI-2
	BOL	56
Tchaikovsky: Waltz from *Sleeping Beauty*	AIM	IV-1

VARIATION FORM

Variation is both a device and a form. As a device, it may be applied to any musical element—rhythm, melody, or harmony—in any of the musical forms. As a form, variation refers to a piece of music that is structured entirely upon the application of variation techniques.

The design of the variation form, known as *theme and variations,* involves the statement of a theme followed by a number of restatements—the variations. The theme is usually in binary or ternary form. The variations retain the basic form of the theme while alterations occur in the melody, rhythm, or harmony; changes in tonality and tempo may also occur.

ANDANTE FROM SYMPHONY NO. 94 (" SURPRISE ")

Additional examples of variation form:

Anderson: "The Girl I Left Behind Me"	AIM	V-2
Caillet: Variations on "Pop! Goes the Weasel"	AIM	IV-1
	BOL	65
Copland: "Simple Gifts" from *Appalachian Spring*	BOL	65
Guarnieri: Brazilian Dance	AIM	VI-2
	BOL	55

SONATA FORM

A *sonata* is a multimovement work for one or two instruments. It usually contains three or four contrasting pieces of large design. A *symphony* is a sonata for orchestra; a *quartet* is a sonata for four instruments; a *quintet* is a sonata for five instruments; a *concerto* is a sonata for a solo instrument and orchestra.

The term *sonata form*, or *sonata-allegro form*, refers to the structural design utilized most frequently in the first movement of sonatas of the above types. It is a large three-part form consisting of *exposition* (A), *development* (B), *recapitulation* (A).

In the exposition the thematic material of the movement is presented. This consists of a *principal theme* and a *subordinate theme* and these themes will often be in one of the smaller part forms. The principal theme is usually vigorous and dramatic in character and is always in the tonic key of the movement. The subordinate theme is generally more lyrical in character and is stated in the dominant key. The exposition may also include a *closing theme* (*codetta*) and *bridge passages* (*transitions*) between the principal and subordinate themes and between the subordinate and closing themes.

157

The development section is devoted to a "working out" of the materials presented in the exposition. This may take the form of presenting fragments of the themes (*motives*) in various combinations and in several keys. The motives may be altered melodically and rhythmically and may be combined in new contexts and into contrapuntal texture. Frequently, only one of the themes may be utilized in this manner, as in the Schubert example below. At the end of the development section there will usually be a *retransition* passage the purpose of which is to reestablish the tonic key in which the recapitulation occurs.

The recapitulation section is essentially a repetition of the exposition. However, in this section the subordinate (and closing theme, if any) must now appear in the tonic key.

Two additional sections are often included in the sonata form, namely an *introduction* and a *coda*. The introduction is usually slow in tempo and only rarely contains reference to materials presented in the exposition. The coda, on the other hand, is quite often based on thematic material; new material may also be introduced, in which case the coda may become quite lengthy.

The sonata-allegro form may be outlined as follows:

Introduction
(optional)

A *Exposition*
- Principal theme in tonic key
- Bridge passage (transition)
- Subordinate theme in dominant key
- Codetta or closing theme

B *Development*
- "Working out" of thematic material
- Retransition to tonic key

A *Recapitulation*
- Principal theme in tonic key
- Bridge passage (transition)
- Subordinate theme in tonic key
- Coda or concluding theme in tonic key

The Schubert example used to illustrate the sonata-allegro form contains the following: (1) a very brief introduction, (2) presentation of principal and subordinate themes (each repeated) both followed by related transition passages, (3) short development on a motive from the principal theme, (4) recapitulation of the two themes with related transitional passages, and (5) a short coda.

SYMPHONY NO. 5 IN B FLAT
(FIRST MOVEMENT)

Schubert
AIM V-1

Principal Theme

Allegro

Subordinate Theme

Additional examples of sonata-allegro form:

Mozart: Symphony No. 40 in G Minor   Standard Recording
Prokofieff: Classical Symphony   Standard Recording

CONTRAPUNTAL OR POLYPHONIC FORMS

The terms contrapuntal and polyphonic are often used synonymously with reference to music that contains two or more rhythmically and melodically distinctive parts or "voices." The combining of such parts is called counterpoint ("point against point"). Polyphonic compositions are usually classified in terms of the contrapuntal techniques that the composer employs in the composition of a musical work and they seldom conform to any set pattern of design. The overall form of a particular composition is always dependent on the musical content rather than on a formalized design. Nevertheless, musicians tend to use the term *form* in discussing contrapuntal music and the most familiar polyphonic forms are the *canon* and the *fugue.*

Canon

A canon is a form in which a melody is imitated strictly by one or more voices after a given time and at a particular interval. The familiar *round* is a type of canon which is always sung or played in unison or octaves by two or more individuals. As a form the canon is not suitable for extended compositions. However, it is frequently employed by composers in brief compositions or in sections of larger compositions. When so used, it is referred to as *canonic imitation*. The Farandole by Bizet listed on page 161 is a good example of the use of this contrapuntal technique.

Fugue

The fugue is a polyphonic composition of two or more voices or instruments which develops a short melodic theme, called a *subject,* through contrapuntal means. A good fugue subject will contain one or more characteristic motives that are readily recognizable.

All fugues begin with an *exposition.* Structurally, this is the most rigid section of this form. Using a four-voiced fugue as an example the exposition would consist of the following:

1. The presentation of the fugue subject alone in one voice in the tonic key.

2. The imitation (*answer*) of this subject in the dominant key, a fifth above or a fourth below.

3. The presentation of a new subject (*counter-subject*) as a continuation of the fugue subject and heard simultaneously with the answer.

4. The restatement of the fugue subject in the tonic key, one octave below the first statement.

5. The answer to this restatement while it continues with the counter-subject.

6. The concluding cadence which is usually on the dominant if the fugue is in a major key or on the tonic of the relative major if it is a minor key.

After the first subject and answer there may be a short transitional passage, *episode,* used for the purpose of modulating into the proper key for the restatement. Also, after the subject and counter-subject have been exposed in any one voice, this voice is free to continue in an unrestricted manner as a *free voice.*

The exposition of a four-voiced fugue may be diagramed thus:

Soprano S_____ CS_ _ _ FV......

Alto   S_____ CS_ _ _ (E) FV......

Tenor   S_____ CS_ _ _ FV......

Bass   S_____ CS_ _ _ (E) Cadence

S—Subject, CS—Counter-subject, E—Episode, FV—Free Voice

Following the exposition the structure of the fugue is usually free, consisting of alternating statements of the fugue subject and episodes in related keys. The episodes may be based on fragments of the subject or counter-subject or upon new material. The fugue subject itself may be altered in different ways, shortened or lengthened, augmented, inverted, and so forth.

Toward the end of the fugue a *stretto* may appear. This is the name given to a passage in which the subject is imitated by another voice before it has been completely stated in the first voice. However, all fugues end with a clear and complete statement of the subject. The final cadence is sometimes preceded by or built upon a sustained tone, *pedal point,* held in the bass independently of the accompanying voices.

LITTLE FUGUE IN G MINOR

Bach
AIM VI-1

Additional examples of polyphonic compositions:

Bach: "Jesu, Joy of Man's Desiring" from Cantata No. 147	AIM	V-1
	BOL	62
McBride: Pumpkineater's Little Fugue	BOL	65
Bizet: Farandole from *L'Arlésienne* Suite No. 2	AIM	VI-1
Thomson: Fugue and Choral on "Yankee Doodle"	BOL	65

11

Style Periods
in Music

Musical style is concerned with the manner and ways in which musical thought is expressed. In order to more fully understand musical styles, it is necessary to be familiar with the main historical periods. Throughout history, artistic expression has been influenced by political, social, and economic forces which have resulted in basic changes in styles. Because these changes are evolutionary some stylistic elements tend to overlap. For example, the years 1800 to 1820 reveal characteristics of both Classical style and early Romantic style. The listener reflects his knowledge of basic styles when he becomes able to respond to music in ways such as, "That sounds like the music of Bach," or "This is music which could have been written in no other time than in our own century." The most widely accepted approach to the study of style is in relation to periods.

The music of the Medieval and Renaissance periods is, perhaps, only of passing interest to the average layman. It was, however, during the twelfth, thirteenth, and fourteenth centuries that the development of many-voiced (*polyphonic*) music, as opposed to one-voiced (*monophonic*) music, took place as well as the movement from modal to tonal music. Composers of the twelfth and thirteenth centuries utilized triple meters and repeated rhythm patterns, while those of the fourteenth century preferred duple meter with less rigid rhythmic treatment. Vocal music predominated although instruments were used. The harmony sounds harsh and bleak to our ears. The music had a thin texture and it was modal. Music of the fifteenth and sixteenth centuries remained polyphonic, but major and minor tonalities grew in popularity among the still dominant modes. This music is easily identified as "not as old," and much of it is acceptable as beautiful music to our twentieth-century ears. Bar lines were seldom used; the music was generally unmetered, that is, the meter signature was not used as it is today. Instead, the stress and rhythm of words governed rhythm and meter with a result that the music was generally smooth and flowing. The polyphony reflected the same basic harmonious concepts we understand today; the rhythm was more complex than that of the earlier music. Imitation was widely used. This is a composer's device in which a melodic idea is restated by another voice or voices in close succession. Palestrina is the best-known composer of this period. Nearly all composers wrote for the church as he did.

Although this earlier music is of interest, music with which we are in contact today is usually of no earlier time than that of the Baroque period.

THE BAROQUE PERIOD (1600–1750)

The beginning of this important period was marked by the emergence of the solo song, apparently in an attempt to balance the emphasis on polyphony which continued throughout the period. These songs were accompanied by bass instruments and early keyboard instruments, notably the harpsichord, and this accompanying part had a *figured bass* (or *thorough bass*) consisting of a written bass line with figures (numerals) that indicated the part the bass instruments were to play and the harmony which was thus directed to be improvised by the harpsichordist. The figured bass is a dominant characteristic of the period and was utilized in many types of music from opera to instrumental pieces. This style of music is called *homophonic*.

These were exciting times in which to live. Great names in science included Newton and Harvey, in literature there were Moliere and Milton, and in art Rubens and Rembrandt. It was an age of expansion, discovery, and exploration, and the arts reflected this with aspects of expansiveness, grandeur, and impressiveness. Opera was created as a new musical form and performed for the public on a lavish scale little known today. Other new forms included the oratorio, cantata, fugue, overture, trio sonata, concerto grosso, and chorale prelude. Instrumental music grew in popularity, but the orchestra was not yet standardized as we know it today, and all manner of instrumental combinations flourished. Sometimes vocalists and instrumentalists performed from the same score in more or less formal presentations. Dance music became music to be listened to as well as danced to; these dances included the sarabande, allemande, and gigue, and they were put together to form the instrumental suite. Among the instruments of that day were the viola de gamba, viola d'amore, lute, recorder, and high-pitched trumpets without valves, for the brass instrument valve was not invented until the nineteenth century.

The old modes were gradually abandoned in favor of the major and minor modes which are dominant in the periods to follow. Polyphony became firmly integrated into the system of major-minor tonality. Since dynamics consisted mainly of loud or soft (the crescendo and decrescendo were not favored, possibly because of the inflexibility of many of the instruments), we are likely to hear clear dynamic levels similar to terraces. The rhythm was steady, with a regular accent that was emphasized by the bass parts. This was the "new rhythm" of that time, and it was in sharp contrast to the unmetered music of the Renaissance period.

Johann Sebastian Bach was the leading composer of the period. He brought Baroque polyphony to its maturity, and the period closes with his death in 1750. Handel was the other great figure in Baroque music. Other important composers include Monteverdi, Purcell, Alessandro Scarlatti, Domenico Scarlatti, Corelli, and Vivaldi.

Summary of Baroque Style

1. Steady rhythm having a modern concept of meters.
2. A firm, solid bass line with figured bass accompaniment.
3. Dynamic levels rather than crescendo and decrescendo, but with no extremes of loud and soft.
4. Major and minor tonalities predominate.
5. Instrumental music tends to feature alternation of solo instruments and strings or groups of instruments.
6. Polyphony predominates.

RELATED RECORDINGS[1]

	AIM	BOL
Bach		
Badinerie from Suite No. 3 in D Major	III-1	
Fugue in G Minor ("Little")	VI-1	
Gigue from Suite No. 2 in B Minor	I-1	
"Jesu, Joy of Man's Desiring" from Cantata 147	V-1	62
Rondeau from Suite No. 2 in B Minor	II-2	
Corelli-Pinelli		
Suite for Strings: Sarabande, Gigue, Badinerie	VI-2	63
Handel		
Fireworks Music:		
Bourée	III-2	55
Menuetto	III-2	
Ground, A		53
Water Music: "Hornpipe"	II	

[1] AIM—*Adventures in Music;* BOL—*Bowmar Orchestral Library.*

THE VIENNESE CLASSICAL PERIOD (1750–1810)

If one had lived in this period, its features would not be as clear to him as they appear to us today, for there were a number of stylistic trends at work. One of these was the *Rococo,* which was in opposition to the grandiose ideas of the Baroque. This style, sometimes called Style Gallant, stressed minute details of ornamentation and sought a delicate elegance on a small scale. The little ceramic figurine as opposed to large and noble statuary seems to typify its spirit. Rococo style abandoned the polyphony of the Baroque in favor of an ornamented homophony. A style trend that appealed to the middle class was called *Empfindsamer Stil* (expressive style); it was most clearly represented by sentimental songs extolling bourgeois virtues. Philosophers emphasized enlightenment—the Age of Reason—and musicians such as Rameau and Beethoven reflected the optimism of the belief that man could ultimately control his environment. Another trend, *Sturm und Drang* (storm and stress) opposed the above ideas and sought philosophical answers in imagination and emotion as opposed to logic and reason, and this emphasis on emotion is believed to be reflected in the music of Haydn, Mozart, and Beethoven. Because cultural life was dominated by the aristocracy, the arts were subservient to the ruling class and became elegant, formalized, restrained, and impersonal. Many composers were employed to serve the aristocratic establishment rather than to serve the churches, as had been common in the past.

Artistic expression with classical characteristics can be found in varying degrees in all periods of history. Classical concepts include restraint, clarity, objectivity, symmetry, and conformity. These were the stylistic concepts that dominated the Viennese Classical period. The beat (pulse) was lighter than the more vigorous Baroque pulsation; rhythm patterns were likewise more light and crisp. Tempi were moderate, with ritardando and accelerando coming into more frequent use. The crescendo-decrescendo idea developed in contrast to the dynamic levels of the Baroque style. Repeated phrases or periods were often performed at dynamic levels contrasting with their first appearance, however; a loud phrase would be repeated more softly, and a soft phrase would be repeated more loudly. There was an effect of simplicity and lightness as compared to the heavier features of Baroque music. Polyphony was generally in the background, with clear, straightforward melodies emphasized. The phrases were likely to be of very regular two- and four-measure lengths. The general design of the music reflected the sophistication of the aristocracy, with form more important than emotion.

The instrumental group at the Mannheim court in Germany evolved to form the basis of the modern orchestra, with its sections of strings, woodwinds, brasses, and percussion. The clarinet was introduced. The piano became the favored keyboard instrument rather than the Baroque harpsichord, and instrumental music became more important than vocal music.

Melodies were often folk-like. The concept of melodic *development* became highly important and was skillfully employed. This concerns the utilization of a melody or its motives in many different ways in the fabric of compositions. The texture was thin as compared to that of late Baroque music or of the Romantic period music to follow. Tonality was firmly established. The sonata-allegro form developed; this form is considered one of man's greatest achievements. The symphony, quartet, and concerto evolved to become established forms. Leading composers include Haydn, Mozart, Schubert, Gluck, and Beethoven, whose music bridged the Classical and Romantic periods.

Summary of Classical Style

1. Elegance, grace, and refinement combined with simplicity, serenity, clarity, and restraint.
2. Formal symmetry and balance that result in an impersonal and relatively unemotional style.
3. Homophonic textures having a very clear melodic line.
4. Employment of a variety of dynamics.
5. Ingenious thematic development.

RELATED RECORDINGS

	AIM	BOL
Gluck		
"Air Gai" from *Iphigenia in Aulis*	I-1	
"Musette" from *Armide Ballet Suite*	II-2	
Haydn		
Surprise Symphony:		
Andante (Theme and Variations)		62
Minuet		63
Mozart		
Menuetto from Divertimento 17 in D	V-2	
Minuet in C		53
Minuet from Symphony No. 40		62
Romanza from *Eine kleine Nachtmusik*	IV-1	
Schubert		
Symphony No. 5 in B-Flat (First Movement)	V-1	

THE ROMANTIC PERIOD (1810–1890)

The aristocratic establishment broke down after the French Revolution, and nineteenth-century liberalism followed. The term "Romantic" is not particularly exact in relation to this period, which contained more crosscurrents of philosophical thought than did the Classical period. It was a time of expansion and ferment not unlike the Baroque period in some of its aspects, e.g., the emergence of a more grandiose style and larger performing groups. When the aristocracy declined, the patronage system in which royalty, nobility, or the church paid composers to write music also declined. This set the composer free to express himself and to hope that the general public—or possibly some wealthy person—would somehow support him in unrestricted artistic endeavors. Thus, although the composer was freed from employer restrictions, he became the victim of economic insecurity, the price he had to pay in order to compose as he pleased. The concert hall became the center of musical activity rather than the palace or the church as in earlier days.

In the general free spirit of the times, rhythm became more free. Syncopation grew in favor, and phrases tended to be less regular than those of the symmetrical music of the Classical period. The moderate tempi of the Classical period were swept away by extremes of fast and slow. *Tempo rubato*[2] reached its full development, and *accelerando* and *ritardando* were used more frequently. Extremes in dynamics were common. Chromaticism and dissonance were increasingly used to give the composer additional means of expression. As the period progressed, harmony became more emphasized as a primary musical element and at the same time came to be less certain about its allegiance to a tonal center. The prevailing texture was thicker and heavier than the clear and light texture of the Classical period. The composer felt unrestricted by older forms and did not permit them to stand in the way of his communication with the listener. While the older forms were modified, there were few new forms other than the tone poem (in which the story dictated the form), the art song, and the rhapsody, a free form. Music for the piano underwent great expansion, moving with mechanical improvements in the instrument.

The music was predominantly homophonic in character, and instrumental melodies were likely to be vocally conceived, as evidenced by the number of them which became popular songs in the twentieth century. The development of harmony which led to the use of tone color as an expressive element was an important aspect. The rise of national schools of composers who attempted to write new music expressive of their particular national culture was a natural result of the "freedom to be different." The music of this period constitutes the largest part of the music played today and is usually better known by the public than that of any other period. Representative composers include Bizet, Brahms, Chabrier, Chopin, Rimsky-Korsakoff, Mendelssohn, Saint-Saëns, Schumann, Tchaikovsky, Verdi, and Wagner.

[2] Flexibility of tempo due to slight accelerandos and ritardandos depending on the performer's or conductor's interpretation of the music.

Summary of Romantic Style

1. Subjective, descriptive, emotional, and nationalistic elements are characteristic.
2. Instrumental tone color is employed to convey feelings and moods.
3. Expansion in harmonic devices includes such aspects as chromaticism and dissonance.
4. Long, flowing melody lines are prominent and often singable.
5. A wide range of emotional expression is evidenced.
6. There are extremes in both tempo and dynamics.

RELATED RECORDINGS

	AIM	BOL
Bizet		
L'Arlésienne Suite No. 2		
Farandole	VI-1	
Minuetto	IV-2	
Brahms		
Hungarian Dance No. 1	V-2	
Hungarian Dance No. 6		62
Chabrier		
España Rhapsodie	V-1	
Dvořák		
Slavonic Dance No. 1		55
Slavonic Dance No. 7	IV-2	
Grieg		
Norwegian Rustic March	IV-1	
Peer Gynt Suite (complete)		59
"In the Hall of the Mountain King"	III-2	
Mahler		
Theme from Third Movement, Symphony No. 1		62
Mendelssohn		
Scherzo from *A Midsummer Night's Dream*		57
Schumann		
Traumerei from *Scenes from Childhood*	IV-2	63
Sibelius		
"Alla Marcia" from *Karelia Suite*	V-1	
Finlandia		60

Tchaikovsky

THE IMPRESSIONISTIC PERIOD (1890–1910)

Although many composers continued to write in the Romantic style, the impressionists reacted against the emotional, descriptive, and texturally heavy music of the late nineteenth century. Like the impressionist painters and the symbolist poets of the day, these composers tried to avoid realism in favor of conveying impressions. The relation between their music and the impressionist painting is striking, for both have a hazy and dream-like quality. Nature is frequently the subject. There is less rhythmic drive and tension present in this style, and there is a lower dynamic level although the conclusion of some of the compositions of Ravel would not agree with this. Harmonic experimentation led to attempts to escape the major-minor tonal system by such means as employing the old modes, the pentatonic and whole-tone scales. Parallel fourths, fifths, and octaves were favored. Systematic chord progressions of the past were not favored as much as individual chords selected for their coloristic effects. Block-like chords were arranged in parallel motion, and there were "escaped chords" which did not resolve, but seemed to "escape" to distant and indistinct tonalities. Tone color was raised to equal status with harmony while melody declined in importance. This musical style can be viewed as a transition from nineteenth-century music to the Contemporary period which follows.

Instruments were employed in new ways; for example, the very low register of the flute was exploited, as was the very high register of the trombone. Mutes were used and the harp was favored; both of these contributed to tone color and special effects: Leading composers included Debussy, Ravel, Delius, Griffes, de Falla, and Respighi.

Summary of Impressionistic Style

1. Melodies tend to be vague; at times they seem to be only remnants of the long and flowing Romantic melodies. Thematic development is almost absent.
2. The tone color is misty, blurred, and pastel in effect. Muted instruments and employment of extreme ranges of instruments contribute to this tone color.
3. The harmony is often unexpected, unresolved, and yields a vague fairy-like atmosphere. A trend away from the major-minor system is evident.
4. The texture is luminous and transparent.
5. The form is often simple, sometimes a series of episodes.

169

RELATED RECORDINGS

THE CONTEMPORARY PERIOD (1910–   )

The most difficult period to analyze is the one in which we live; there has not been sufficient lapse of time to be able to "see the forest for the trees." However, certain generalizations can be made. We have seen the gradual abandonment of the major-minor tonality which began in the late nineteenth century become an actuality in the Contemporary period. Although some composers of stature continue to utilize traditional harmony, many others have found it to be inadequate for them. In its place we find some of the music constructed on arbitrary "tone rows" which avoid any reference to major and minor scales. The old modes are sometimes utilized, as are Oriental scales and some heretofore overlooked scales found in folk music of some Western countries. Dissonance has been employed to such an extent that the distinction formerly existing between it and consonance is blurred. Some composers experiment with microtones, scale steps smaller than the traditional half step. Polytonality combines two or more keys (tonalities); polyrhythm combines two or more rhythms or meters. Polyphony again interests composers, and the old techniques of the past are revived in new harmonic settings that are often dissonant. Chords are constructed as composers choose to build them, and it is common to find them as a series of fourths or fifths rather than as a series of thirds that was a cornerstone of the old harmony. Some Classical trends can be seen, such as objectivity (less emotionalism) and a thin, clear texture. Rhythm has become much more complex with what might be a partial return toward the unmeasured and unmetered music of the Renaissance period. There is often a strong rhythmic drive, a great deal of tension, and a mechanical aspect of style that opposes the Romantic rubato style of the nineteenth century. Unorthodox instrumental combinations remind the listener of those of the Baroque period.

The freedom of the composers to compose as they please seems to be complete. They no longer rely on the church, the aristocracy, or on wealthy patrons. Most composers of today are employed as college teachers, librarians, and in other occupations; they are seldom employed as composers. Thus, most of them are free to compose whatever they like in a manner somewhat similar to the scientist in a laboratory who does pure research. For example, one of the most advanced composers of his day was Charles Ives, who made his living in insurance and composed the music he wanted to compose after his day's work was done. The best of these composers have mastered the styles and techniques of the music of the past so that they can draw upon all of these resources in the creation of the "new music." Added to these are new resources of this century which include musical instruments such as those invented by Harry Partch, and electronic music which utilizes sounds placed on tape and sounds programed through computers. Composers include Bartók, Ginastera, Kodály, Villa-Lobos, Shostakovich, Stravinsky, Schöenberg, Ives, Schuller, Stockhausen, and many more.

Summary of Contemporary Style

1. A mixture of styles is to be found.
2. A strong trend toward avoiding traditional major-minor tonality is evident.
3. The texture is likely to be thin.
4. Melodies are often fragmentary and angular; they tend to be instrumentally conceived.
5. Dissonance is emphasized in both harmony and counterpoint.
6. Bitonality and polytonality (two or more keys at once) are often employed.
7. The rhythm tends to be irregular, energetic, and insistent; it may be polyrhythmic.
8. The style is experimental, unemotional, and impersonal.

	AIM	BOL
Bartók		
Hungarian Sketches:		
"Bear Dance"	III-2	
"Evening in the Village"	V-2	
Copland		
"Circus Music" from *Red Pony Suite*	III-1	
"Hoe-Down" from *Rodeo*	V-2	55
"Simple Gifts" from *Appalachian Spring*		65
Ginastera		
"Wheat Dance" from *Estancia Ballet* Suite	IV-1	
Guarnieri		
Danza Brasiliera	VI-2	55
Ives		
Fifth Movement from Symphony No. 2		65
Kabalevsky		
The Comedians Suite:		
Pantomime	I-1	
March	III-1	
Gallop	III-1	
Gavotte		55
Intermezzo		55
Waltz	I-2	
Khatchaturian		
Masquerade Suite:		
Mazurka		55
Gallop		55
Waltz	IV-2	
Kodály		
Hary Janos Suite:		
"Entrance of the Emperor"	IV-2	81
"Viennese Musical Clock"	II-1	81
Menotti		
Suite from *Amahl and the Night Visitors:*		
Introduction		58
"March of the Three Kings"		58
"Dance of the Shepherds"	IV-2	58

172

Some examples should be sought from other sources such as Folkways FT 3612, "Twelve-Tone Music" and Folkways FX 6160, "Sounds of New Music" which includes Cowell's tone clusters, Cage's prepared piano, Varése's isolation of rhythm, electronic music, and multiple tape music.

12

Instruments and Voices

In the preceding chapter there were references made to the evolution of instrumental music which culminated in the large nineteenth-century orchestra. In this evolution two influences reacted upon one another: the trends in musical styles and the mechanical improvement of the instruments. The instruments of the orchestra are capable of producing a stunning array of tone colors and fascinating gradations of dynamics, pitch, and tone quality. As complex as all this is, the musical capabilities rest upon a number of simple scientific facts. Sound is produced by vibration. The faster the vibration, the higher the pitch; the slower the vibration, the lower the pitch. The quality of sound is affected by the materials from which the instrument is constructed, the shape of resonating chambers, and the manner in which the sound is produced.

The symphony orchestra is comprised of four sections: the strings, the woodwinds, the brasses, and the percussion. Even a rudimentary knowledge of instruments that comprise these sections will enhance your enjoyment in listening to instrumental music.

THE STRINGS

The instruments of the violin family and the harp comprise this section. The members of the violin family look alike except for their size. The smallest is the violin; the viola is slightly larger. Both are held up with the left hand and bowed with the right. The cello is sufficiently large so that it must rest on the floor with the player sitting down to play it. Largest is the double bass (string bass); the player either stands up to play it or he sits on a high stool.

The string sound is made by bowing or plucking the strings, causing them to vibrate. The bow is made of coarse hair mounted on a wooden frame. Rosin is placed on the hair and this substance causes the friction that makes the strings vibrate. Thin, short strings produce high sounds, and long, thicker strings produce lower sounds. The player's fingers have the effect of shortening or lengthening the vibrating parts of the strings, thus producing different pitches.

The harp has forty-three strings and seven pedals which are used to adjust the strings to the proper key needed. The harp's strings are stroked or plucked to produce the sound. The player sits on a chair to play this large instrument.

THE STRINGS: (A) violin, (B) viola, (C) cello, (D) string bass. *Photograph courtesy of Bowmar Records, Inc.*

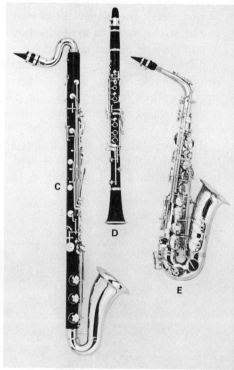

THE WOODWINDS: (A) flute, (B) piccolo, (C) bass clarinet, (D) clarinet, (E) saxophone. *Photographs courtesy of Bowmar Records, Inc.*

THE WOODWINDS

The piccolo and flute are played by blowing across a mouth-hole to produce what is called an "edge tone." The air is directed to the edge of the hole by the lips. The piccolo is the highest-pitched instrument of the woodwinds, as might be expected from its tiny size. The flute is twice the length of the piccolo, thus it is pitched one octave lower. The oboe, English horn, bassoon, and contra bassoon are played with double reeds, while the clarinets

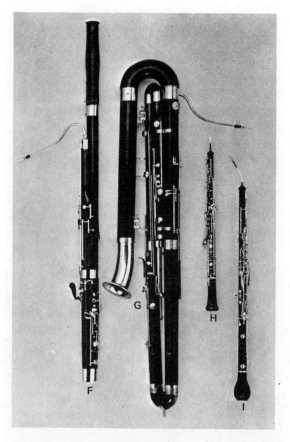

THE WOODWINDS (*cont.*): (F) bassoon, (G) contra bassoon, (H) oboe, (I) English horn. *Photograph courtesy of Bowmar Records, Inc.*

and saxophones are played with single reeds. The contra bassoon sounds the lowest pitches of any instrument in the orchestra. Both the clarinet and saxophone are members of the same family and there are different sizes of each instrument. The saxophone is more popular in the band than it is in the orchestra, but it is used in the orchestra occasionally. Although saxophones and most flutes and piccolos are not made of wood, they are still classified as woodwind instruments.

THE BRASSES: (A) trumpet, (B) French horn, (C) tuba, (D) trombone. *Photograph courtesy of Bowmar Records, Inc.*

THE BRASSES

The brass instrument player produces sound by vibrating his lips against a cupped mouthpiece. The valves on the trumpet, French horn, and tuba detour the vibrating air column into shorter and longer tubing to raise or lower the pitch. Another influence on pitch production is the degree of tension or relaxation in the player's lips; the greater the tension, the higher the pitch, The trumpet is the highest pitched brass instrument and the tuba is the lowest. The trombones have no valves. Their slides accomplish the same purpose as valves on the other brasses by shortening or lengthening the vibrating air column. Some brass instruments such as the baritone and melophone are used exclusively in bands. The Sousaphone is a type of tuba designed for the marching band.

THE PERCUSSION

Vibrations that produce sound from percussion instruments are set in motion by striking. There are three classifications of percussion instruments: those on which a membrane is struck, those which are solid, and those which are of the keyboard type. The keyboard type instruments and the tympani

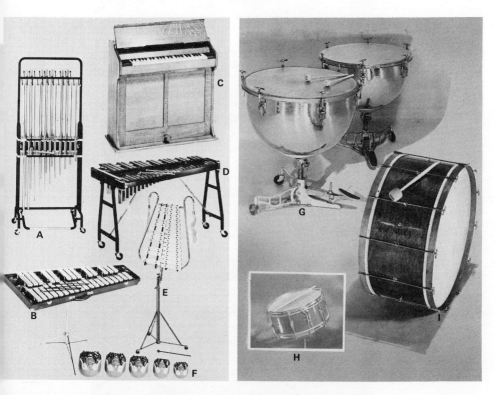

PERCUSSION INSTRUMENTS: (A) chimes, (B) glockenspiel, (C) celeste, (D) xylophone, (E) glockenspiel, (F) temple blocks, (G) tympani, (H) snare drum, (I) bass drum. *Photographs courtesy of Bowmar Records, Inc.*

have definite pitch; the others do not. The percussion section also includes a number of special effect devices, from bird whistles to anvils, too numerous to mention.

Membrane	Solid	Keyboard
bongo drums	castanets	celeste
conga drums	claves	chimes
bass drum	cymbals	orchestra bells
snare drum	gong	(glockenspiel)
tambourine	maracas	marimba
tympani	triangle	piano
(kettledrums)	wood block	xylophone

PERCUSSION INSTRUMENTS (*cont.*): (J) gong, (K) maracas, (L) castanets, (M) triangle, (N) cymbals, (O) tambourine, (P) woodblock. *Photograph courtesy of Bowmar Records, Inc.*

Courtesy The New York Philharmonic Society.

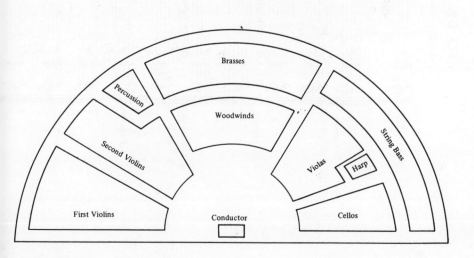

OVERTURE
TO DIE MEISTERSINGER VON NÜRNBERG, EXCERPT

(Sehr mässig bewegt)

Wagner

(Wagner: Overture to *Die Meistersinger von Nürnberg*, Excerpts) of Hardy and Fish's *A Workbook for Analysis—Music Literature, Volume I: Homophony*

183

VOICES

As wonderful as the modern instruments are, there is no instrument which can equal the appeal of singing voices. Voices, with their imperfections, are after all, *human,* while the instruments are at best artistic tools to use.

Voices are classified in accordance with their range and quality. The most broad classifications are simply soprano and alto for women and tenor and bass for men. There are, however, a number of subdivisions of these classes, as shown below.

Approximate Vocal Ranges

The above average ranges do not depict the true range of many of the voices described below which may exceed the approximate ranges by wide margins.

Adult Voice Classifications

Coloratura Soprano:	The highest range; a very agile voice.
Lyric Soprano:	Light, high voice, not as agile as coloratura.
Dramatic Soprano:	A heavier voice with more theatrical quality.
Mezzo Soprano:	Darker quality of tone; rich low range.
Contralto:	The lowest female voice; somewhat heavy in quality.
Lyric Tenor:	Highest male voice, very light in quality.
Dramatic Tenor:	A heavier tenor voice with more theatrical quality. Sometimes called "Tenor Robusto."
Baritone:	Has range of a bass, but quality reminiscent of tenor.
Bass:	The lowest male voice; an exceptionally low voice is sometimes called "Basso Profundo."

RECORDINGS FOR STUDY

Instruments

Bowmar Records	*Meet the Instruments* (Filmstrips and pictures available)
Capitol Records	*Instruments of the Orchestra* (Narration by Yehudi Menuhin)
Decca Records	*The Symphony Orchestra*
Folkways	*The Orchestra and Its Instruments*

Jam Handy	*Instruments of the Symphony Orchestra* (Filmstrips available)
RCA Victor Co.	*Instruments of the Orchestra* (Pictures available)
Vanguard	*Instruments of the Orchestra* (Narration by David Randolph)

Voices

Coloratura Soprano	Delibes: "Bell Song" from *Lakmé* Handel: "Rejoice Greatly" from *Messiah*
Lyric Soprano	Handel: "Come Unto Him" from *Messiah* Villa-Lobos: *Bachianas Brasilieras No. 5*
Dramatic Soprano	Mozart: "Dove sono" from *The Marriage of Figaro* Wagner: "Dich, Teure Halle" from *Tannhäuser*
Mezzo Soprano	Bizet: "Habanera" from *Carmen* Offenbach: "Barcarolle" from *Tales of Hoffmann*
Contralto	Bach: "Herzliebster Jesu" from *St. Matthew Passion* Handel: "He Was Despised" from *Messiah*
Lyric Tenor	Handel: "Every Valley" from *Messiah* Rimsky-Korsakoff: "Song of India" from *Sadko*
Baritone	Bizet: "Toreador Song" from *Carmen* Handel: "Where E'er You Walk" from *Semele*
Bass	Handel: "Why Do the Nations" from *Messiah* Moussorgsky: "Farewell of Boris" from *Boris Godunov*

A

Hand Signals

These drawings show the hand signals as they appear to the person making them.

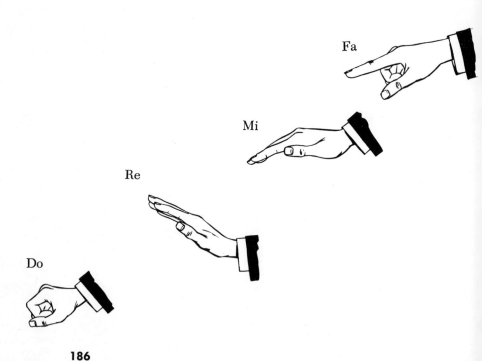

Fa

Mi

Re

Do

Do

Ti

La

So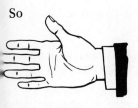

187

B

The Recorder

The recorder is the ancestor of the modern flute. It was a popular instrument during the Renaissance, the Baroque, and the early Classical periods. Purcell, Bach, and Handel are among the many early composers who wrote excellent music for the instrument, and contemporary composers and folk musicians are using it today. It is a popular instrument in elementary and secondary schools throughout the world.

The four different recorders used today form a family.

Soprano (descant)	tuned in C
Alto (treble)	tuned in F
Tenor	tuned in C
Bass	tuned in F

The instruments most widely used in the schools are those tuned in the key of C, the soprano and the tenor. The soprano has the advantage of low cost, and both can play music directly from the song books at the pitch indicated. However, the musically superior instrument is the alto (treble), tuned in F. It is recommended to those who will study the instrument seriously. Its advantages are its excellent tone quality combined with a more dependable tone production than the soprano.

However, most people begin their study of the recorder with the inexpensive soprano (descant) in C. The Baroque (English) fingering is preferred to the German because its use results in playing better in tune, thus only the Baroque fingering will appear here. Careful listening to pitch is essential to playing the instrument well. It helps to sing and play songs alternately so that the mental images of the pitches are reviewed and strengthened. Breath pressure is of vital importance, for the soprano can be easily overblown. Generally speaking, blow *gently*. By controlling breath pressure the player can control intonation.

The solid dots in the fingering chart on p. 192 are closed holes and the white dots are open holes. The half-closed circles require some explanation. When this symbol is used for the left thumb, it means to use the thumbnail in the hole in a manner that closes 90% of that hole. In this position the thumb is bent at a right angle with the hole, the flesh covers the largest part of the hole, and there is a small space left between the nail and the upper edge of the hole. This is called "pinching the octave" because the partly closed hole is used to produce pitches an octave higher.

Beginning to Play

Hold the instrument with the left hand uppermost (nearest the mouth), with the thumb closing the thumb-hole at the back, and the first three fingers covering the highest three holes. The four fingers of the right hand cover their respective holes, with the thumb helping to support the recorder as it is played. Holes to be closed must be airtight, for leakage produces unwanted sounds.

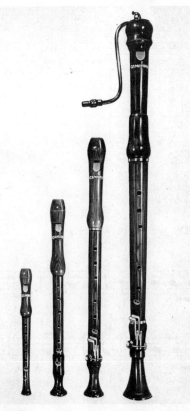

Soprano, Alto, Tenor, and Bass Recorders. *Photograph courtesy of Trophy Music Company.*

Begin your practice of playing the recorder with the tones available by using the fingers of the left hand only. These tones should be mastered before proceeding to those that involve use of the right hand fingers. The five songs notated on the following pages provide an easy approach to learning to play the recorder.

Preparing to blow gently, start the tone with the tip of the tongue as if saying "doo." Stop the tone with the tip of the tongue by bringing it behind the upper front teeth to stop the breath from entering the instrument.

HOT CROSS BUNS

Hot cross buns, hot cross buns.

One a pen - ny, two a pen - ny, hot cross buns.

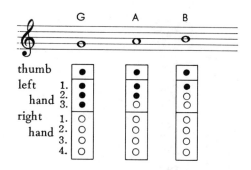

MERRILY WE ROLL ALONG

WHISTLE, DAUGHTER, WHISTLE

GO TELL AUNT RHODY

LOVE SOMEBODY

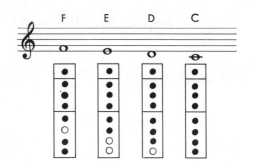

HOT CROSS BUNS

Next, play the songs in Chapter 1 as notated. As you continue playing through the book, refer to the fingering chart whenever necessary.

BAROQUE (ENGLISH) FINGERING FOR SOPRANO RECORDER

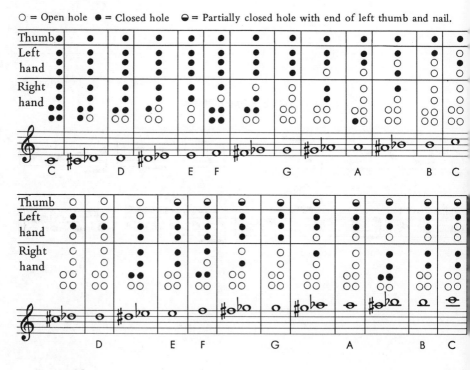

C

The Guitar
and Ukulele

THE GUITAR

The standard guitar has six strings. Its fingerboard has *frets,* metal strips that mark off the spaces where the player places his fingers. Each fret represents one half-step in pitch. The six strings are numbered from the lowest pitched to the highest.

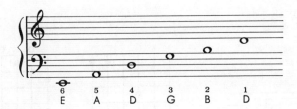

THE UKULELE

The ukulele is a four-stringed instrument that evolved in Hawaii from the Portuguese guitar. Two tunings are in common use.

The frets and strings are numbered as follows:

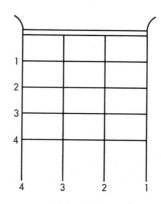

BASIC CHORDS

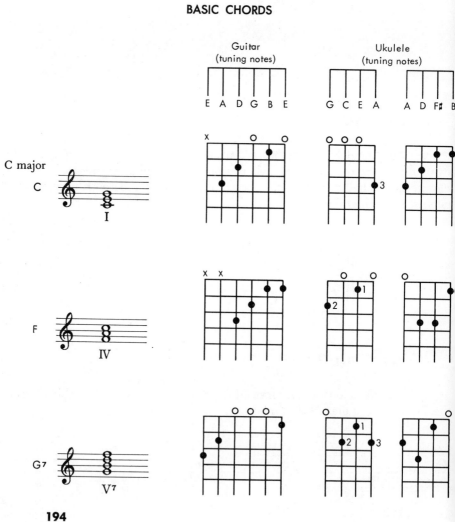

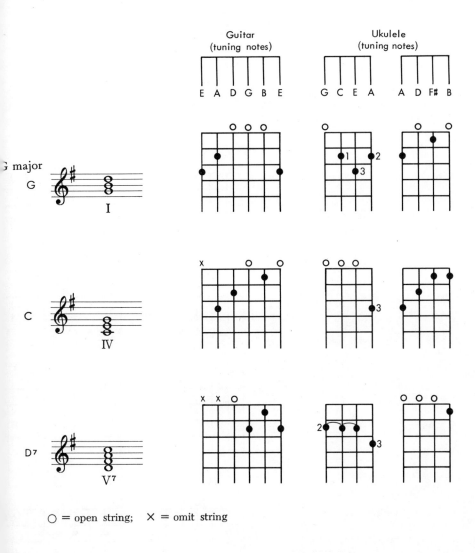

G major
G

I

C

IV

D⁷

V⁷

○ = open string;   X = omit string

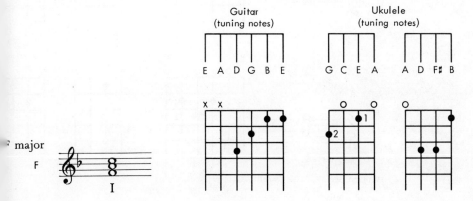

F major
F

I

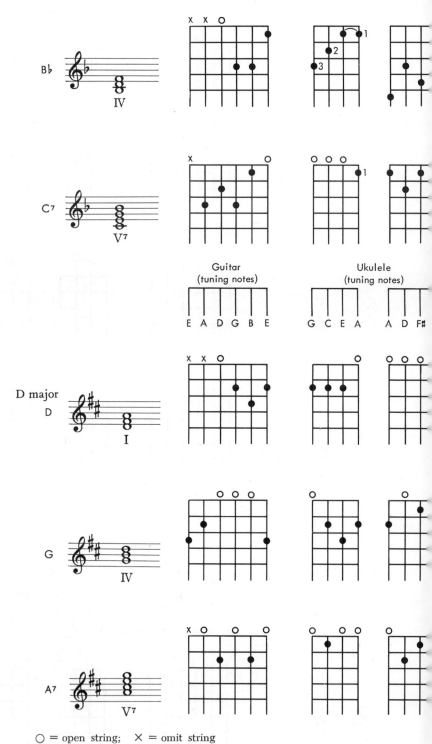

O = open string; X = omit string

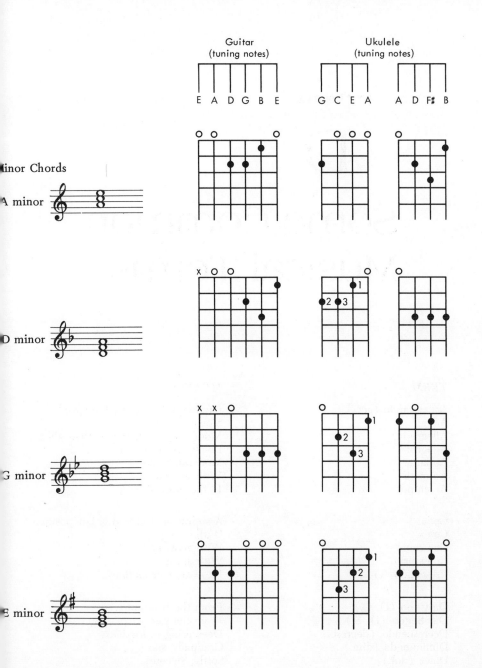

Minor Chords

A minor

D minor

G minor

E minor

O = open string;   X = omit string

D

Some Common Musical Terms

TERM	MEANING
Accelerando (accel.)	Gradually increasing the speed
Adagio	Slowly, leisurely
Allegretto	Moderately fast, slower than allegro
Allegro	Lively, brisk, rapid
Andante	Moderately slow
Animato	With animation
A tempo	In the original tempo
Coda	A supplement at end of composition
Con	With
Con moto	With motion
Con spirito	With spirit
Crescendo (cresc.)	Increasing in loudness
Da Capo (D. C.)	From the beginning
Dal Segno (D. S.)	From the sign
Decrescendo (decresc.)	Decreasing in loudness
Diminuendo (dim.)	Gradually softer
Dolce (dol.)	Softly, sweetly
Espressivo	With expression
Fermata	Hold (prolong)
Fine	The end
Forte (f)	Loud

Fortepiano (fp)	Accent strongly, diminishing
Fortissimo (ff)	Very loud
Grandioso	Grand, pompous, majestic
Grave	Very slow
Largo	Broad and slow
Legato	Smoothly, the reverse of staccato
Lento	Slow, between andante and largo
Maestoso	Majestically, dignified
Mezzopiano (mp)	Moderately soft
Moderato	Moderately
Pianissimo (pp)	Very softly
Piano (p)	Softly
Presto	Very quick
Rallentando (rall.)	Gradually slower
Ritardando (rit.)	Gradually slower and slower
Ritenuto	In slower time
Sforzando (sf)	Forcibly with sudden emphasis
Sostenuto	Sustained, prolonged
Staccato	Detached, separate
Tempo	Movement, rate of speed
Tranquillo	Quietly
Troppo	Much
Un poco	A little
Vivace	Bright, spirited
Vivo	Lively, spirited

E

Patriotic Songs

AMERICA

Samuel Francis Smith

Henry Carey (?)

1. My coun - try, 'tis of thee, Sweet land of lib - er - ty,
2. My na - tive coun - try, thee, Land of the no - ble free,
3. Let mu - sic swell the breeze, And ring from all the trees
4. Our fa - thers' God, to Thee, Au - thor of lib - er - ty,

Of thee I sing. Land where my fa - thers died! Land of the
Thy name I love. I love thy rocks and rills, Thy woods and
Sweet free-dom's song. Let mor - tal tongues a - wake; Let all that
To thee we sing. Long may our land be bright With free-dom's

Pil - grims' pride! From ev - 'ry — moun - tain - side, Let — free - dom ring!
tem - pled hills; My heart with — rap - ture thrills Like — that a - bove.
breathe par - take; Let rocks their — si - lence break, The — sound pro - long.
ho - ly light; Pro - tect us — by Thy might, Great — God, our King!

AMERICA THE BEAUTIFUL

Katherine Lee Bates   Samuel A. Ward

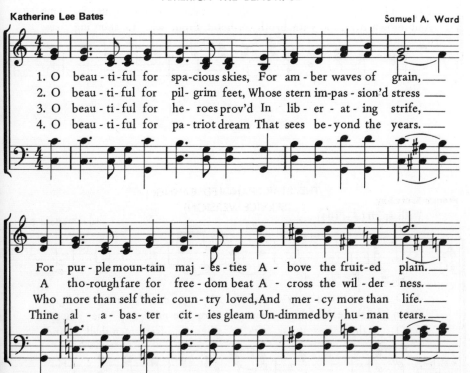

1. O beau - ti - ful for spa - cious skies, For am - ber waves of grain,—
2. O beau - ti - ful for pil - grim feet, Whose stern im - pas - sion'd stress —
3. O beau - ti - ful for he - roes prov'd In lib - er - at - ing strife,—
4. O beau - ti - ful for pa - triot dream That sees be - yond the years. —

For pur - ple moun - tain maj - es - ties A - bove the fruit - ed plain.—
A tho - rough - fare for free - dom beat A - cross the wil - der - ness. —
Who more than self their coun - try loved, And mer - cy more than life. —
Thine al - a - bas - ter cit - ies gleam Un - dimmed by hu - man tears. —

A - mer - i - ca! A - mer - i - ca! God shed His grace on thee,____
A - mer - i - ca! A - mer - i - ca! God mend thine ev -'ry flaw,____
A - mer - i - ca! A - mer - i - ca! May God thy gold re - fine,____
A - mer - i - ca! A - mer - i - ca! God shed His grace on thee,____

And crown thy good with broth - er-hood, From sea to shin-ing sea.
Con - firm thy soul in self con-trol, Thy lib - er - ty in law.
Till all suc-cess be no - ble-ness, And ev -'ry gain di - vine.
And crown thy good with broth - er-hood, From sea to shin-ing sea.

THE STAR-SPANGLED BANNER
(SERVICE VERSION)

Francis Scott Key

With spirit ($\quad = 104$)

John Stafford Smith

1. O____ say! can you see, ____ by the dawn's ear- ly light,
2. On the shore, dim -ly seen____ thru the mists of the deep,
3. O____ thus be it ev - er when____ free men shall stand,

What so proud-ly we hailed at the twi-light's last gleam-ing?
Where the foe's haught-y host in dread si-lence re - pos-es,
Be - tween their lov'd homes and the war's des-o - la-tion!

Whose broad stripes and bright stars, thru the per - il - ous fight,
What is that which the breeze, o'er the tow - er - ing steep,
Blest with vic - t'ry and peace, may the heav'n-res-cued land

O'er the ram-parts we watch'd, were so gal-lant-ly stream-ing?
As it fit-ful-ly blows, half con-ceals, half dis - clos-es?
Praise the Pow'r that hath made and pre-served us a na-tion!

And the rock - ets' red glare, the bombs burst-ing in air,
Now it catch-es the gleam of the morn-ing's first beam,
Then — con-quer we must, when our cause it is just,

203

Gave__ proof thru the night__ that our flag was still there.
In full glo - ry re - flect-ed now__ shines on the stream;
And __ this be our mot - to: "In __ God is our trust! "

Chorus ♩=96 *f*

O __ say, does that __ Star-Span-gled Ban - ner__ yet __ wave __
'Tis the Star - Span-gled__ Ban - ner, O long may__ it __ wave __
And the Star - Span-gled __ Ban - ner in tri- umph shall __ wave __

broaden *ff*

O'er the land __ of the free and the home of the brave?
O'er the land __ of the free and the home of the brave!
O'er the land __ of the free and the home of the brave!

Index of Songs

Index of
Instrumental
Compositions

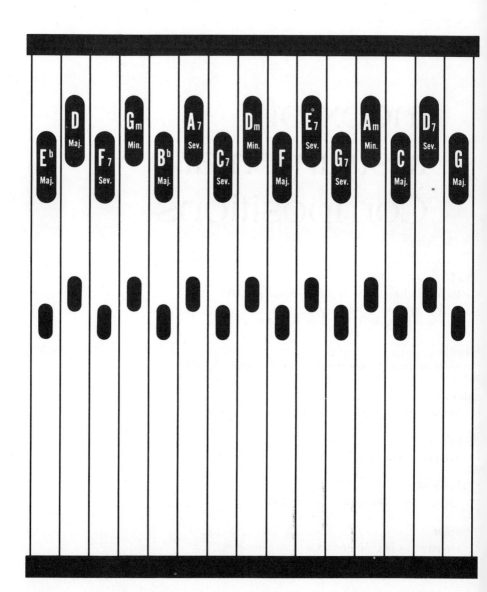

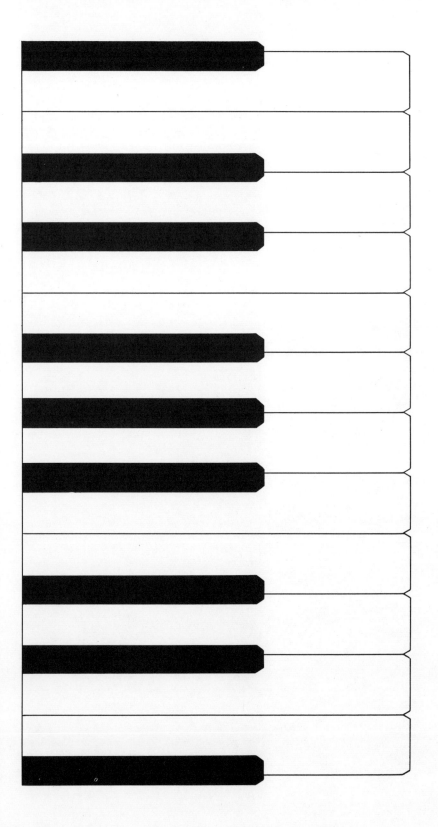

Index

211